SEVERELY RETARDED CHILDREN: WIDER HORIZONS

DAN D'AMELIO
American Education Publications

SEVERELY RETARDED CHILDREN: WIDER HORIZONS

CHARLES E. MERRILL PUBLISHING COMPANY
Columbus, Ohio *A Bell & Howell Company*

THE SLOW LEARNER SERIES
edited by Newell C. Kephart, Ph.D.

International Standard Book Number: 0-675-0922-5

Library of Congress Catalog Card Number: 74-147053

1 2 3 4 5 6 7 8 9 10 - 75 74 73 72 71
Printed in the United States of America

Foreword

The question of curriculum development in classes for the trainable mentally retarded has presented a problem to special education for sometime. On the one hand there is the question of realistic goals which will be socially and/or economically useful but which will fall within the limits of ability possessed by these children. On the other hand is the demand by parents and school personnel for accomplishment in "readin, ritin and rithmetic." A very searching question asks how useful any social or economic skill can be in our complex modern society without at least a modicum of the traditional academic learnings.

Exclusive concern with the first of these approaches has frequently led to the teaching of nothing but "self help" skills. Although these learnings are undoubtedly necessary in maintaining the child in any situation, institutional or community, in which he may be placed, they do not appear to be a legitimate function of the public school system as that program has traditionally been conceived. On the other hand, exclusive concern with the second approach has frequently led to continued pressure for academic learnings which are not possible in the face of the unresolved learning deficits displayed by the child. We therefore, see many classroom programs for trainable mentally retarded which are either unrelated to traditional school objectives or are drastically watered down versions of normal classroom curriculum.

In the present volume, the author has attempted to bridge the gap between these two extremes. He presents a curriculum involving basic academic learnings while at the same time concerning himself with social accomplishments. Academic material is graded to the abilities to be expected from the child and where deficits occur in areas essential to the learning these are dealt with first before further academic skills are pursued. The reader will recognize many therapeutic procedures recommended in previous volumes in this series among the recommendations in the present volume. Instead of waiting until all deficits have been remediated, however, the present author proceeds with teaching as soon as the child demonstrates those skills essential to the particular task at hand. Such a combination of therapy and teaching represents a great economy of time and assures that successful remediation will be translated into academic accomplishment.

The author suggests, by implication if not directly, that his is a terminal academic program. He does not propose to start teaching and go as far as he can in the traditional texts, giving up when further progress seems improbable. Rather he recognizes the limitations of his group and sets about to teach, within these limitations, a limited body of skills which will be most useful in relation to its quantity. His recommended vocabulary list is a case in point. These words have been carefully selected to permit the child to do as much as possible with the relatively few words which he can be expected to master. "If this is as far as we can expect to go," he seems to say, "let's move in those directions which produce the greatest yield per unit of progress, recognizing that a terminal point in the learning is to be expected." The result is a curriculum of reasonable expectations of completion and maximum utility upon completion.

It is hoped that this volume can help to set the pattern for a more logical and more effective curriculum for the trainable mentally retarded and that through such development education for these children can become more meaningful.

N. C. Kephart, Ph.D.

Glen Haven Achievement Center
Fort Collins, Colorado

Preface

The purpose of this manual is to 1) show that the severely retarded child is capable of learning; 2) to suggest that his present education is inadequate; 3) to place him in the perspective of potential, rather than functioning level; 4) to point out his present physical limitations and suggest ways of overcoming these limitations; 5) to inspire educators, particularly classroom teachers, toward further curriculum development; 6) to provide realistic hope for parents; and 7) to have educators, administrators, and psychologists reappraise their ideas about the education of severely retarded children.

This manual avoids using the term "trainable" for those children whose I.Q. is below 50. This term, the writer believes, does the severely mentally retarded child an injustice. The term "trainable" is both offensive and inaccurate. The severely retarded child is not only capable of training; he is also capable of *learning.*

As a group, educators believe that severely retarded children can learn to do very little, if any, academic work. This manual suggests that *if special methods are used,* many severely retarded children can learn, at least, the fundamentals of reading, writing, and arithmetic.

Educators also believe that, in view of the severely retarded child's future dependence (or semi-dependence), academic skills would serve no practical purpose. This may or may not be true. However, the writer believes that *giving a child the opportunity to learn basic academic skills will have an important bearing on his future.* If a child is not treated as an infant, but as a student, is not given playthings, but the same kind of schoolwork as his brother or sister, and is not given a substitute-parental upbringing, but a basic education, *he will more likely develop the self-confidence that is essential to meet the persistent demands of daily living.*

Teaching basic academic skills to severely retarded children is not simply a matter of transferring a set of techniques from one group of children to another. Traditional techniques for teaching these skills, although successful with normally intelligent children, are inadequate for severely retarded children, since they need procedures that break learning experiences into smaller units. The methods presented in this manual attempt to meet this problem.

Although the methods are essentially experimental, it does not mean they have little or no validity. Their successful results, in terms of academic and motor development, justify their inclusion in this manual. But, by no means are these methods definitive. We have a long way to go, and it will take the efforts of many.

What may be said to be at the "heart" of special education is the problem of teaching basic skills that most children learn on their own *to children who cannot attain these skills independently*. This, of course, is a unique problem in the field of education. It means going back to the "child behind the child," that is, developing basic, pre-school skills *in school-age children*.

The teacher, therefore, deals with basic causes. If a child cannot read, write or do arithmetic, the teacher goes beyond the immediate problem to basic, "non-academic" skills. A child cannot deal with symbolic material until he has the necessary perceptual abilities; nor can he deal with the manipulative demands of academic work unless he possesses certain visual-motor abilities. In short, academic skills are dependent upon basic perceptual-motor skills.

Training severely retarded children in perceptual-motor skills, therefore, is essential to their education. Guided by other books in the Slow Learner Series, the teacher should conduct perceptual-motor activities as an integral part of the children's academic development.

Acknowledgements

Were it not for Dr. Newell Kephart, this book would probably still be on my bookshelf in manuscript form. Whatever its weaknesses, I assume full responsibility; whatever its strengths, I gratefully attribute to Dr. Kephart's guidance and inspiration. To my "editor-in-residence," my wife Fanny, I express in print my gratitude for her wise counsel, her unfailing patience, and her long hours of typing. My thanks go to Gail Palmer, production editor of Charles E. Merrill Publishing Co., for "going beyond the call of duty"—quite often, it seemed, she was more of a collaborator than an editor. My thanks also to Bernard Kelly of the Boy Scouts of America, Middlesex County Council, Middletown, Connecticut, for his help and cooperation.

For my successful photo-hunting expeditions, I gladly acknowledge the courteous cooperation of Mary Z. Gray of the President's Committee on Mental Retardation in securing the photographs on pages 2, 22, 24, 46, 61, 74, 90, 106, and 110; Norman Subotnik of the Division of Mental Retardation, H.E.W., in obtaining the photographs on pages 6 and 105; the administrative staff of the Mansfield Training School, Mansfield Depot, Connecticut, in securing the photographs on pages 36, 52, and 80; Robert Ruffner of the President's Committee on Employment of the Handicapped; and Paul Thompson of the Bureau of Handicapped, U.S. Office of Education.

I also acknowledge my indebtedness to the "children in the classroom down the hall" for teaching me more than I could ever teach them.

This book is dedicated to my mother and father.

Contents

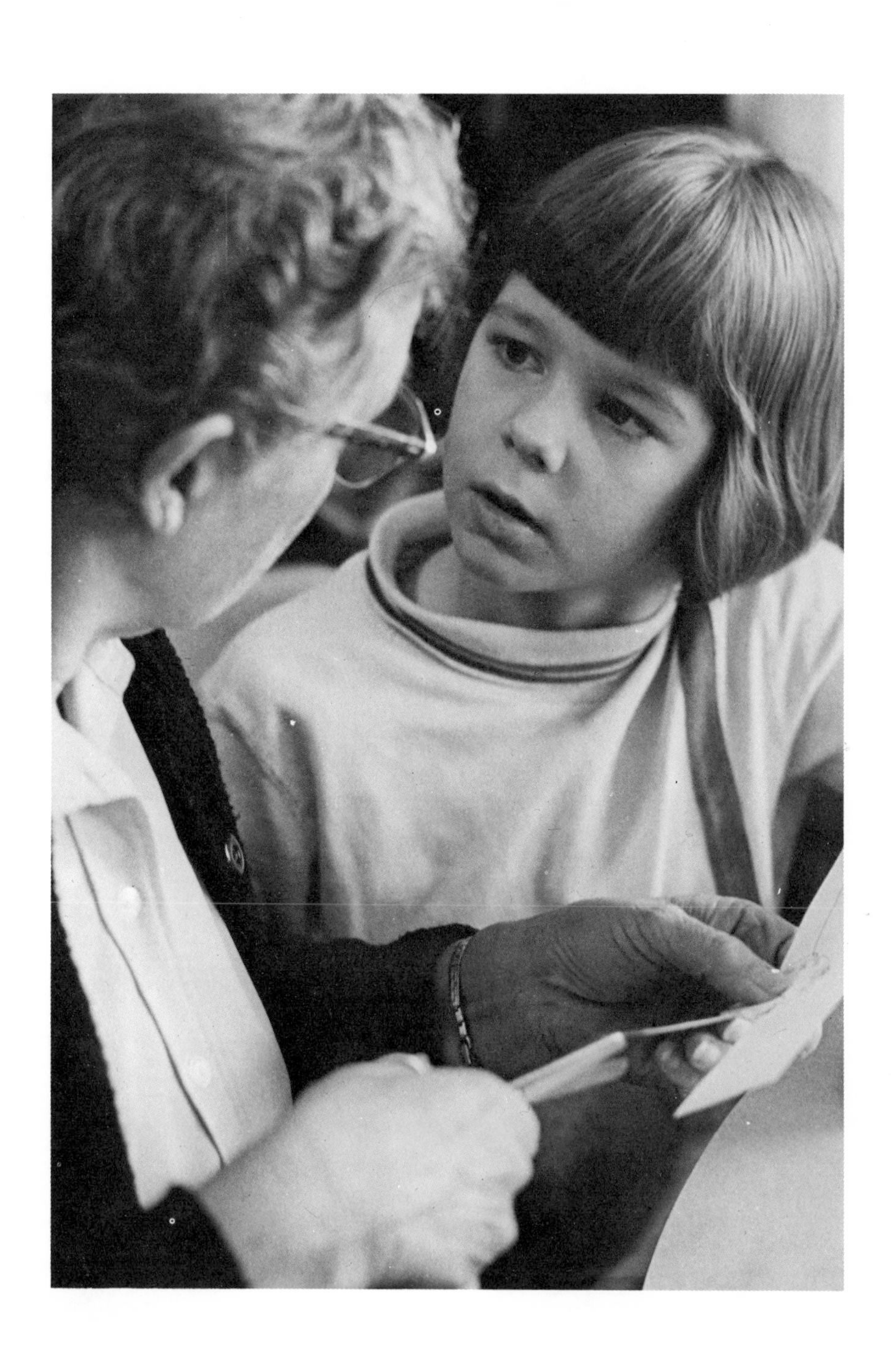

section 1

Academic Skills

The main effort in behalf of mentally retarded children has been in terms of institutionalized care. Institutions were our first answer to the problems they posed. About one hundred years ago, we began setting up institutions for their "shelter, instruction, and improvement."

At about the turn of this century, public schools entered the picture. For the most part, they modeled their programs on those of private schools, which had pioneered in the field. Today public school classes for the *moderately retarded* are found in a majority of the states.

The severely retarded child was not discovered by public education until about mid-century. Except for several cities, such as, St. Louis and New York, public school programs for severely retarded children were nonexistent before mid-century. In 1950, the National Association for Retarded Children was formed; rapidly, thereafter, public school doors began to open to severely retarded children.

Within five years, legislation for the education of "trainable severely mentally retarded" children had been passed in 19 states, and by 1960, the majority of the states had recognized the problem. In 1961, there were approximately 17,000 severely retarded children attending public school classes. In 1966, the number had increased to 64,800; and today the number is estimated to be 100,000.*

In contrast to the rapid public school enrollment of these children is the near static history of their curriculum. For two decades the public school curriculum has remained essentially unchanged; it still mirrors the training offered by institutions a century ago. The emphasis continues to be on training in self-care and social adjustment, with the children learning such habits as washing, dressing, clothing care, appearance, safety, and good manners.

Thus, the severely retarded child traditionally has been trained to be an inoffensive personality who will venture forth from school and mix with society without any undesirable habits. Theoretically, after public school training, a severely retarded child can be trusted not to pick his nose in company, to smile prettily when introduced, to hang his coat, to brush his teeth, to refrain from spitting at children who tease, and to blow his nose.

Of course, the severely retarded child needs training in self-care and social adjustment. But does this emphasis do justice to the child's potential? Suggestions that the children are getting less than an adequate education run into formidable opposition. For years the tendency among educators has been to "stand pat" and not to question their basic assumptions. Few indeed have been the voices that have expressed dissatisfaction with the curriculum. The disciples of status quo have comfortably held their ground. Of course, they permitted minor changes and adjustments in the curriculum, but the basic point of view has remained unchanged: the severely retarded child is not educable.

The philosophy of "noneducability" is based on judgments regarding the child's academic abilities. The following statements indicate the tenor and scope of these judgments:

The children will not succeed in an academic program.

Older severely retarded children can learn to recognize their names, and read signs such as "stop," "go," "danger," and "walk"—beyond this level the children do not read.

The children can only learn to write their names—little else.

All that can be expected from these children is that they learn to count to five in a life situation.

How valid are such judgments?

We live in pressing times, we are pushed into judgments and formulations, the need overrides discretion, and expediency supplants research.

*Based on figures from the National Center for Educational Statistics.

Our guesses become theories, our narrow-mindedness becomes dogma, our ignorance becomes a curriculum, our complacency becomes conviction. The result: a series of "authoritative" pronouncements without benefit of practical knowledge. These pronouncements, if taken seriously, have a profound effect on the pattern of education for the severely-retarded child.

This field is amply endowed with so-called authorities, including psychologists, doctors, and educators, who have one thing in common—their lack of actual experience in teaching severely retarded children. Theirs is the "knowledge" of bias, and it is unfortunate that their voices tend to drown out the minority of those who have either practical knowledge or an open mind. This point is made with some force since it has considerable bearing on both the present status of education for the mentally retarded and future possibilities for enlarging its scope.

We cannot determine the limitations and potentialities of a child solely in a psychologist's, a doctor's, or even an educator's office. These questions are ultimately decided in a classroom. We cannot know in advance what a child can or cannot do until we give him a chance to learn. I.Q. and other standardized tests cannot indicate how far a given child may be expected to go and at what rate. The only valid prognostic instrument is the teacher with skill and patience. To her, there is no such thing as a poor subject. If a child does not respond to one approach, she tries another until she finds the modality in which the child can successfully function and develop. This does not require only one week or one month of effort, but a long period of hard and patient work on the part of the teacher.

The case studies presented in this manual cover a wide range in terms of I.Q. and mental and chronological ages. Thus, they represent more than a fair percentage of the severely retarded children presently receiving an education in public, day training, private, and state schools. (It should be pointed out that most of the case studies came from lower middle income families.) In presenting the case studies, the sex, general appearance, etiology, chronological and mental age, and I.Q. of each child is given, but further data, such as psychological and social background, is excluded, since basically the children are typical of the severely retarded children receiving an education today.

chapter 1

The Child's Potential

In a public school system on Long Island, New York, a class for "trainable" severely retarded children was formed. In the course of the first four and a half years the class was taught by three successive teachers, each of whom followed the traditional approach in their work with the children, emphasizing training in self-care and social adjustment. Academic skills were never part of the children's curriculum. In March of the fourth year, the third teacher resigned, and the writer was asked to take over the class.

The first weeks were spent in establishing discipline, order and routine. At first, the nine children in the class found it very difficult to remain seated; they preferred wandering about the room, playing in the sandbox, and sitting on the floor with games, as they had been doing. The children also had difficulty in adjusting to the teacher (the writer) as the authority figure, since one of the boys, a big, strapping mongoloid—dowsyn*—teenager, insisted on acting as a sort of "straw-boss." In addition, the children found it difficult to function as a unit because of the eleven-year span in their chronological ages (5 to 16). Gradually, however, *with continued persistence on the teacher's part,* the class began to take on the

*The term "mongolism" was first used by J. Langdon Down in 1866. As a clinical designation, the term is unscientific and inaccurate and, as a label for children, the designation has unfortunate overtones. Therefore, the writer suggests a new term, one that is based on the newer, medical designation for this condition, Down's Syndrome. By using the first three letters of each word, the word *dowsyn* is formed; thus, instead of a mongoloid, a *dowsyn* child.

appearance of a formal learning situation. The children remained in their seats, the focus of authority was clearly on the teacher, and specific procedures were established.

After almost a month's time, a formal learning situation had been reached, and the question foremost in the teacher's mind was what he should establish as objectives of the program. The teacher had few preconceptions about either the limitations or potentialities of severely retarded children; his teaching experience had been limited in depth, but extensive in scope, having taught normally intelligent children on elementary, junior and senior high levels, and mentally retarded children at a private institution. Primarily, however, his had been an academic background. Thus, having been given a free hand in developing the curriculum,* it was natural that he would reflect this kind of background in his work with the children. About the third week, with little confidence in the idea, the teacher suggested that his students bring notebooks the next day.

The following day the children could not get off the school bus fast enough; five of them had notebooks, and two of them were carrying bright, new school bags.

The first academic skill the class attempted was writing. Each morning the children quietly opened their notebooks and, according to their varying abilities, began to either scribble or form letters. The first writing objective was learning to write their names. Gradually, the scribbles became lines, and the crude letters became readily distinguishable. Alan G., a tall hunched twelve-year-old dowsyn boy with a slight brain injury, a mental age of three years five months, and an I.Q. of 27†, in the beginning could form only the letter **A**; in three weeks he had learned to write his full name without copying it and without assistance.

Because of Alan's achievement and the more modest achievements of several of his classmates and in response to their obvious interest, the teacher decided to take the children as far in academic work as their interest and abilities would allow. How far that would be, the teacher did not know, but there would be no pressure from the teacher for the children to achieve. Following this guideline, academic skills were included in the children's program for the next two years. It was the children's enthusiasm which determined to what extent and at what tempo a given academic area was studied.††

---

*This "free hand" in developing a curriculum was never explicitly sanctioned by the administration; it would be more accurate to say that the administration simply didn't care what transpired in the classroom, as long as the children were "contained."

†The Stanford Binet tests were used for all the children.

††Several of the children in the class had normally intelligent brothers and sisters attending the same school and undoubtedly this contributed to their motivation.

MARCH 1960 TO JUNE 1960

During the final quarter of the school year, the children followed an essentially pre-academic program. (The pre-academic work was *part* of the curriculum, which also included arts and crafts, music, and recreation.) On the basis of the teacher's observation, it appeared that the children were able to follow a regimentation of pre-academic activities which included:

1. Pencil control
2. Drawing basic lines
3. Coordinating eye-hand movement
4. Identifying people, places and things in pictures
5. Listening to a story and following the story line
6. Associating oral words with their printed counterparts
7. Recognizing quantitative differences (*big* and *little, many* and *few, high* and *low, etc.*)

The academic work took up about one hour of a five hour school day and was done daily. The children spent 15 to 20 minutes on each academic area: reading, writing, and arithmetic. Writing, which was usually done first, began with the children opening their notebooks to their homework. (A homework assignment was given each day.) After the homework had been checked, the children proceeded to the day's lesson. Letters, words

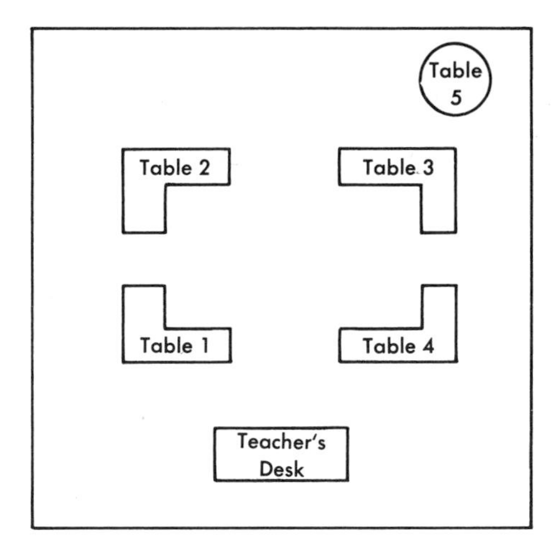

FIGURE 1-1. Seating Arrangement

or names were written on the chalkboard to be copied by the children at their desks.

Actually, the children did not use desks, but tables which had been in the room when the writer took over the class. Using the tables was quite advantageous as it turned out, and they were used for the next two years. The children used four right-angled tables and one round table. The arrangement of these tables in the classroom is shown in figure 1-1.

This table arrangement proved helpful for two reasons: it permitted easy maneuverability about the classroom, and it provided a ready-made arrangement for group work. With this seating arrangement, the teacher could easily supervise the children at their work, and he could conveniently group the children in any subject area. Also, the children seemed to derive a sense of security from working at a table with another child, but, at the same time, they perhaps felt a sense of privacy since there were not more than two children to a table.

In the first months, the seating arrangement for the students was as follows:

At table 1 sat two dowsyn boys, both of whom seemed to have more academic ability than the other children. They were Alan P., a short, high-strung, ten-year-old boy with a mental age of four years six months and an I.Q. of 46, and Ed K., a husky, well-coordinated, fourteen-year-old boy with a mental age of six years four months and an I.Q. of 43.

At table 2 sat two brain-injured girls; the younger girl functioned on a much higher level than the older girl. They were Irene S., a dark, heavy-set, sixteen-year-old brain-injured child with severe emotional disturbance, a mental age of five years six months and an I.Q. of 32, and Maria N., a thin, undernourished, twelve-year-old girl with a mental age of five years nine months and an I.Q. of 46.

At table 3 sat two dowsyn children, the girl tending to dominate ("mother") the boy. They were Lois P., an obese, unkempt, sixteen-year-old girl with a mental age of three years seven months and an I.Q. of 22, and Thomas F., a short, husky, eight-year-old boy with a mental age of three years one month and an I.Q. of 37.

At table 4 sat Alan G.

At table 5 sat two brain-injured boys, both of whom were possible schizophrenics. They were Michael S., a non-verbal, highly distractable, eight-year-old boy with a mental age of two years six months and an estimated I.Q. of 30, and Anthony S., an excitable, deeply withdrawn, five-year-old boy with a mental age of three years six months and an estimated I.Q. of 46.

The children at tables 1, 2, 3, and 4 participated in academic work; Michael S. and Anthony S., at table 5, did not.

For a period of about three months, the six* children in the "academic" group participated in pre-academic activities; and by the end of the term, on the basis of samples of the children's writing during this period, it appeared that four children in this group had acquired one or several basic writing skills.

By the end of the term, Lois P., who had never been to school before this year, was able to write her first name. In the beginning she had only scrawled with a pencil. After several weeks she was able to form the letter L ; approximately a month later she was able to write LO ; after approximately another month she was able to write LOI ; and by June 15, she was writing LOIS on page after page of her notebook.

Alan G., by the end of the term, was able to write his full name, and he was able to write from dictation approximately half the letters of the alphabet. Too, it seemed to the teacher that his writing had gained in clarity and control.

Alan P. was able to form several letters in the beginning. In about two weeks he was able to write his first name and in another two weeks his full name. By the end of the term, Alan was able to write all the letters of the alphabet and to copy words and sentences from the chalkboard.

Irene S., in the beginning, was also able to form several letters. Within a few weeks she was able to *copy* her first name and several words from the chalkboard. By May 5, she could copy all the letters of the alphabet and write her first name without copying it. (Irene seemed to have more pencil control than the three dowsyn children, Alan P., Alan G., and Lois P.)

SEPTEMBER 1960 TO JUNE 1961

By the beginning of the new school year the make up of the class had altered. Seven of the nine students of the previous term were still in the class; the two who had not returned were Anthony S. and Maria N. There were three new students, each dowsyn: Rafi S., an energetic, non-verbal, six-year-old boy who was not testable; Susan M., a well-coordinated, highly verbal, five-year-old girl with a mental age of three years three months and an I.Q. of 49; and Haydie N., a shy, non-verbal, eleven-year-old girl with a mental age of two years seven months and an estimated I.Q. of 30.

In September, after the interim of the summer holiday, Lois P. could still write her first name; Alan G. was still able to write his full name and,

*Maria N. had left in April.

as during the previous term, about half the letters of the alphabet; Alan P. could still write his full name and all the letters of the alphabet; but, Irene S. appeared to have difficulty remembering how to write her name. It will be noted that the three children who evidenced retention were dowsyns.

In the first few months of the school year the make up of the class changed again. Susan M., who left in October, was replaced by another very young dowsyn girl, Janice G., a small, friendly six-year-old with a mental age of two years one month and an I.Q. of 34. Michael S., who left in November, was replaced by another brain-injured boy, Richard S., a highly distractable, non-verbal eight-year-old with a mental age of two years nine months and an I.Q. of 30.*

During the school year, the students who participated *as a group* in academic work were the six students who had engaged in academic work the previous term: Ed K., Alan G., Irene S., Alan P., Thomas F., and Lois P. Haydie N., who sat at table 2 with Irene S., did not participate in any academic work because of her inability to relate to others. Janice G., who sat at table 4 with Alan G., attempted pencil control and the drawing of basic lines. Richard S. and Rafi S., both of whom sat at table 5, did not participate in any academic work for the same reason as Haydie N. During the reading, writing, and arithmetic lessons, Haydie N., Janice G., Richard S., and Rafi S. generally used visual-motor materials such as peg boards, wooden puzzles, and beads.

During the school year, on the basis of the teacher's observations and diagnostic tests, it appeared that the children in the academic group were able to follow a program of academic activities that included:

1. The copying of words from a beginning writing vocabulary list (see p. 47)
2. The copying of phrases and sentences (see pp. 49-50)
3. The spelling of words from the beginning writing list
4. Identifying words from the beginning writing list
5. Reading pre-primers
6. Studying concepts of space, size, number, and time
7. Reading, writing, and using numbers

The reading and writing performances of three of the children is indicated by Charts 1 and 2.

---

*All the children were from a single school district.

CHART 1. Reading Performance of Three Dowsyn (Mongoloid) Boys (December 19, 1960 to June 7, 1961)

	Dec. 19	Feb. 24	March 15	April 11	May 10	June 7
Alan P. age 11	Pre-primer II P. 39 (Scott, Foresman)	Pre-primer III P. 34 (Scott, Foresman)	Pre-primer III P. 45 (Scott, Foresman)	Pre-primer III P. 59 (Scott, Foresman)	Pre-primer II P. 61 (Row, Peterson)	Primer P. 10 (Row, Peterson)
Ed K. age 15	(absent)	Primer P. 46 (Scott, Foresman)	Pre-primer II P. 39 (Row, Peterson)	Pre-primer II P. 56 (Row, Peterson)	Pre-primer III P. 43 (Row, Peterson)	Pre-primer IV P. 10 (Row, Peterson)
Alan G. age 13	Pre-primer I P. 33 (Scott, Foresman)	(absent)	Pre-primer II P. 11 (Scott, Foresman)	Pre-primer II P. 39 (Scott, Foresman)	Pre-primer III P. 1 (Scott, Foresman)	(absent)

On December 19, Alan P. was on page 39 of Pre-primer II, which he had been given a few weeks earlier. A month later, (not shown on the chart) he was on page 58 of Pre-primer II. In five more weeks, Alan had finished Pre-primer II and was on page 34 of Pre-primer III. Several weeks later, he was on page 45 of Pre-primer III, and a month later, he was on page 59 of the same pre-primer. In another month's time, Alan had: 1) finished Pre-primer III (the last basic reader of the Scott, Foresman series); 2) completed Pre-primer I of the Row, Peterson series; and 3) reached page 61 of Pre-primer II (Row, Peterson). In still another month's time, Alan had finished Pre-primers II, III, and IV, and he was on page 10 of the Primer (Row, Peterson).

Ed K. had received reading instruction from his mother prior to the time the class began its reading program. His reading experience had been limited to one series, Scott, Foresman, and he had been unable to get through the primer of this series. For these reasons, the teacher decided to introduce him to a different series, Row, Peterson. Approximately 30 words, or about half of the vocabulary words in the Row, Peterson series, were words that were not in the Scott, Foresman series.

On March 15, Ed had finished Pre-primer I, which he had been given earlier in March, and he was on page 39 of Pre-primer II. A month later, he was on page 56 of the same pre-primer. In another month, he had finished Pre-primer II and had reached page 43 of Pre-primer III. In still another month, he had finished Pre-primer III and was on page 10 of Pre-primer IV.

On December 19, Alan G. was on page 33 of Pre-primer I, which he had started a few weeks earlier. In three months, he had finished Pre-primer I and was on page 11 of Pre-primer II. In two more months, he had completed this pre-primer and had begun on Pre-primer III.

CHART 2. Spelling Performance of Dowsyn Boys
(December 7, 1960 to May 26, 1961)

Ed K., age 15

Dec. 7	Dec. 19	Jan. 10	Jan. 19	Jan. 27	Feb. 22	March 20	April 11	May 26
mother	play	mother	mother	mother	mother	mother	mother	mother
father	sleep	father	father	father	father	father	father	father
play	go	go		sleep	play	play	play	play
sleep	car			dog	I	sleep	dog	sleep
go					dog	dog	car	dog
					car	car	house	car
					we	house	toy	house
					go	toy	stop	toy
						go	go	go
						I	to	I
						to	I	and
						my		no
								to
								is
								work
								we
								my
								hello
								the
								school
								love

Alan G., age 13

Dec. 7	Dec. 19	Jan. 10	Jan. 19	Jan. 27	Feb. 22	March 20	April 11	May 26
(none)	(none)	dog	car	(absent)	mother	mother	mother	mother
					father	father	father	father
					play	play	play	play
					sleep	sleep	sleep	sleep
					dog	car	dog	dog
					car	go	car	car
					go	and	toy	we
					work	I	I	my
					and	house	and	teacher
					I	to	to	is
						no	work	the
						toy	hello	today
								work

Alan P., age 11

Dec. 7	Dec. 19	Jan. 10	Jan. 19	Jan. 27	Feb. 22	March 20	April 11	May 26
mother	mother	mother	mother	mother	mother	mother	mother	mother
father	father	father	father	father	father	father	father	father
go	go	go	play	play	play	play	play	play
	sleep	dog	dog	sleep	sleep	sleep	sleep	sleep
	dog	car	car	dog	dog	dog	dog	dog
		stop		car	car	car	car	car
				toy	toy	stop	house	house
				go	go	we	toy	toy
				stop	we	I	stop	stop
					I	house	go	go
					my	toy	I	I
						and	and	and
						no	no	no
						to	to	to
						in	in	in
						work	work	work
						my	we	we
							my	my
							hello	hello
							teacher	teacher
								is
								the
								school
								today
								bus
								love

Chart 2 shows the spelling performance of three dowsyn boys. The chart is based on spelling tests given to the children. The spelling tests were conducted in the traditional manner with the teacher dictating the words and the children writing them on their papers. The words in the chart are from the beginning writing vocabulary list (see p. 47), which the children earlier in the term had copied from the chalkboard into their notebooks. (By the end of the school year, the above three dowsyn boys also had copied into their notebooks all the phrases, sentences, and paragraphs listed on pp. 49-50.)

The counting performance of five of the children is indicated by Chart 3.

No intensive effort was made to teach this group of children to count in a life situation prior to the first date in the record, February 21, and no formal effort was made during the period covered by the chart to instruct the children in counting objects. The number work during the school year had chiefly centered on the use of kindergarten number books, which included numbers 1 to 10.

CHART 3. Counting Performance with 29 Objects

	Feb. 21	April 11	May 15	May 25
Alan P.	29	27	27	29
Ed K.	9	29	29	26
Alan G.	17	14	15	18
Irene S.	5	—	12	12
Thomas F.	2	2	9	10

SEPTEMBER 1961 TO FEBRUARY 1962

During this period of time academic work was continued as part of the curriculum, but its forward motion was impeded by lack of adequate instructional material. In reading, there were no suitable primers. The primers of the pre-primer series represented a large step forward from the pre-primers. For example, in the 1956 edition of the Scott, Foresman series there are 58 vocabulary words in the three pre-primers, but the primer introduces 100 new words. This edition included a "junior" primer. which, in addition to reviewing the 58 pre-primer vocabulary words, introduces 10 vocabulary words of the primer. In the beginning of the school year, Alan G., Alan P., and Ed K. were given *Billy's Friends,** a social studies primer. This primer introduced a large number of new words, and in November, another primer was substituted, *First Steps to Health.*† This primer also introduced a large number of new words. The essential problem in reading materials seemed to be a lack of primers or readers which represented smaller steps forward in terms of new words and concepts. Of course, the children could have been introduced to different pre-primer series, and this the teacher attempted; but, it soon became evident that motivation suffered since the children felt that they were going back to "baby" books instead of going on to "real" books.

In writing, the problem arose of building on the beginning writing vocabulary list (see p. 47), which the children had already studied. In developing this vocabulary list, the teacher had tried to select those words

---

*Alta McIntre and Wilhelmina Hill, (Chicago, Illinois: Follet Publishing Co., 1957).

†Oliver E. Byrd, M. D., et al, (River Forest, Illinois: Laidlaw Bros., 1960).

that represented concepts close to the children's experiences and to include words which would make it possible for the children to write phrases and sentences with only those words from the list (see pp. 49-50). In addition, the teacher had compiled a complete vocabulary list of 100 words (see p. 47), which would be meaningful to the children at some time in their lives. The problem was what criteria were to be used in selecting words for this complete vocabulary list as a *logical and unified* development of the beginning writing list.

In arithmetic, the initial problem was finding a means of developing basic arithmetic concepts of size, number, space, and time; the literature was understandably meager in these areas, since normally intelligent children usually have an understanding of these concepts before coming to school. For about a month, in the beginning of the school year, the children worked with a kindergarten text, *Kindergarten Fun,* published by McCormick-Mathers, which presented a few concepts of space such as *in, out* and *left, right.* As for formal arithmetic—addition and subtraction —the traditional method of drill with its emphasis on memorization of formulas (one and one are two, etc.,) seemed inadequate in terms of comprehending the quantitative relationships involved, and first grade arithmetic texts were too advanced for the children in terms of the written directions for the problems and the pace of developmental sequence. The Cuisenaire System (see pp. 54-55), with its concrete, kinesthetic approach to the teaching of arithmetic, seemed particularly suitable for the children; however, it had been devised and developed for normally intelligent children. Thus, it was necessary to follow a procedure of adaptation which proved to be a slow, laborious process.

Despite these difficulties, the children continued to follow a program of academic activities that included:

1. The copying of phrases and sentences based on the children's day-to-day experiences, e.g., Today is Friday. We go to gym today. I like gym.
2. Reading primers.
3. Working with Cuisenaire rods.

As in the previous school year, academic work was given every day along with homework. The children spent from twenty to thirty minutes on each academic area—reading, writing, and arithmetic.

The children who participated in academic work were Ed K., Alan P., Alan G., Thomas F., Jim M., and Ronald M. (for data on the latter two boys, see p. 18). Lois P., who had participated in academic work from March 1960 to June 1961, did not return in September 1961.

Irene S. was still in the class, but she did not participate in academic work. She had been with the class since March 1960, and her academic accomplishment from that date until June 1961 had been limited to learning to write her name, recognizing a few pre-primer words, and counting up to 12 objects. Irene evidently had more academic ability because she scored "average" on both first grade arithmetic and reading readiness tests.*

Rafi S., Ricky S., and Janice G. were no longer in the class. They had been transferred to another class in the school district that had been formed in September 1961 for younger "trainable" children. Their places were taken by three new students: Carol G., a poorly coordinated, obese, eleven-year-old dowsyn girl with a mental age of three years three months and an I.Q. of 46; Ronald M., a highly distractable, tense, ten-year-old brain-injured boy with a mental age of four years three months and an I.Q. of 43; and Jim M., a thin, highly distractable, eight-year-old brain-injured boy with a mental age of three years five months and an I.Q. of 38 (the latter two boys were brothers). Carol G. withdrew from the class in November, and she was replaced by Michael S., who had been in the class at an earlier date.

The academic accomplishments of the children during the period from September 1961 to February 1962 were as follows.

Thomas F., who had worked with a reading readiness book the previous year, was given Pre-primer I of the Scott, Foresman series in October 1961; he finished this pre-primer about three months later, on January 15, 1962. In six weeks, by February 28, he had finished Pre-primer II and was on page 10 of Pre-primer III. Also, Thomas, who had been able to write only his name prior to March 1960, had learned to write the alphabet during the new term and was readily copying words and phrases from the chalkboard.

Both Ronald and Jim M. had received virtually no formal education prior to their enrollment in the class.† In September 1961, Jim was unable to read or write. On September 9, he was given Pre-primer I (Scott, Foresman series); he finished this pre-primer seven weeks later, on October 30. In about three months, he had finished Pre-primers II and III. During this same period, Jim was able to copy the alphabet and to write his first name.

In September, Ronald was unable to form any letters or to identify any words. Within five months, he was able to identify eight pre-primer words.

---

*The New York Test of Arithmetical Meanings and the First Year Readiness tests (for use with the Row, Peterson series); both tests were administered by the teacher.

†Theirs had been a record of repeated failure and rejection in school and long periods of non-attendance.

As for writing, in about seven weeks, by November, he was able to copy the alphabet, and three months later, he could write his first name and copy words from the chalkboard.

The academic performances of Alan G., Alan P., and Ed K., during the period from September 1961 to February 1962 were chiefly characterized by their retention in reading, writing and counting. During this time no formal reading, spelling or counting lessons were given by the teacher. On December 19, 1961, about six months after their last reading lesson, Ed could identify 22 pre-primer vocabulary words; Alan P. could identify 51 pre-primer vocabulary words; and Alan G. (who had lost his set of last term's reading cards) was able to read sections picked at random by the teacher from the previous year's pre-primers.

Chart 4 shows the spelling retention of the same three boys. The last spelling lesson these boys had was in June 1961; Chart 4 is based on a spelling quiz given about seven months later.*

CHART 4. Spelling Retention of Three Dowsyn Boys

Alan P.	Ed K.	Alan G.
go	go	go
toy	toy	toy
dog	car	car
sleep	dog	dog
play	sleep	play
father	play	father
mother	father	mother
I	mother	no
and	I	to
no	and	work
in	to	we
work	work	teacher
we	we	is
my	is	the
teacher	school	today
is	today	
the	bus	
school	love	
today		
like		
love		

*The 30 words of the beginning writing list were dictated for the quiz (see p. 47). The reader may wish to compare this chart with Chart 2.

About five months after their last counting lesson, Alan P., Ed K., and Alan G. could count 30, 27, and 17 pegs, respectively (out of 30 pegs); this may be compared with Chart 3.

The following handwriting samples of the above three boys are from a spelling quiz on ten words given on February 8, 1962.

ALAN G.
MOTHER
FATHER
PLAY
SEEP
DOG
CAR
ALLY
TOY
STP
GO

ALAN P.
MOTHER
FATHER
PLAY
SLEEP
DOG
CAR
HOUSE
TOY
STOP
GO

EDWARD K.
MOTHER
FATER
PLAY
SLEER
DOG
CAR
HOVES
TOY
SOP
GO

FIGURE 1-2. Writing Samples of Three Dowsyn Boys

SUMMARY

In the two-year period from March 1960 to February 1962, a total of 17 severely retarded children were enrolled in a public school class for periods ranging from one month to two years; of this number, nine participated in academic work for periods ranging from two months to two years, and six made substantial progress in academic skills. The success of these six students in academic work suggests that retarded children *can at least* do first grade academic work, provided that special methods are used.

The writer is not suggesting that the severely retarded child's curriculum be academically oriented. But, he is suggesting that under current policies, educational limitations, which are not entirely realistic, are too often imposed on severely retarded children. Practical experience indicates more constructive approaches. Granted, the writer's data are limited, but at least they strongly imply that a sound curriculum might well include basic academic skills.

All children are entitled to an education that will make them dependable, *self-respecting* citizens, and all children are entitled to an education to the limit of their capabilities. These are basic tenets of our educational system.

chapter 2

Reading

What should be the specific aims of a reading program? Quite simply, to develop basic reading skills. These may include learning to read the alphabet; identifying the child's own name; reading simple signs; developing a sight vocabulary; a basic understanding of letter sounds; learning to read in left to right sequence; learning to read phrases and simple sentences; and learning to read aloud with feeling and understanding.

These goals are modest, indeed, and they are attainable for many of the children. The methods of reaching these goals are outlined in this chapter. They are not necessarily the best methods; however, they have all been used by the writer in his work with children. Their varying degrees of success justify their inclusion in this manual. Teachers are invited to find new and better methods of teaching reading to severely retarded children.

THE ALPHABET

A knowledge of letters will help students in the recognition of words. A knowledge of letter sounds – phonics – should be taught *after the students have acquired a basic sight vocabulary.*

A suggested way of introducing the alphabet is to have the letters prominently displayed in the classroom. They may be tacked or taped above the chalkboard or, on another wall of the room. It is recommended that the letters be placed at the front of the room, above the chalkboard, since they will more readily be seen there than in any other place in the room. This location is also convenient for the teacher — she can remain in front of the room as she points to the letters.

The teacher may use printed letters or make her own using plain newsprint paper or oak tag. The letters should be at least four inches high.

In the beginning, you should present but one new letter in each lesson; later, when the students have learned to identify a number of letters, you may introduce several new letters at a time. Help the students see the shape of each letter. For example, "This is the letter A ." Point to the letter. "See how the letter A is made." Trace the shape of the letter with a pointer. The children also may trace the letters on raised-surface, textured alphabets (see p. 44).

It is important that the children have ample opportunities to say the letters since vocalizing helps learning. For example: slowly and distinctly identify a series of letters; then have the students as a class identify the letters (as you point to each letter); next, call on individual students to name the letters.

For each lesson, you should review the letters which the children have been previously taught. Once the review is completed – and only then – should you introduce the new letters.

It is suggested that you work with capital letters since they are easier for the student to identify.* Later, if you wish, you can teach lower-case letters.

In addition to letters displayed in the classroom, you will use the chalkboard. You will find it a very useful aid. The general procedure is as follows: write a series of letters on the chalkboard; identify the letters; then have the children name the letters as you point to each one.

It is important that the children be asked to read the letters both forward and backwards; if this is not done, the children may very likely "learn" the letters by rote. In writing the letters on the chalkboard, make certain that the letters are large enough to be read easily by the students. Many dowsyns have poor vision. Proceed slowly and never take anything for granted.

Encourage class participation. For example: write the letter L on the chalkboard, then say, "Yesterday we learned this letter." Point to it, "What is the name of this letter?" Then, when it has been identified, "Now I will write another letter." Write the letter M. "This is our letter for today. Do you know what we call this letter?" After it has been identified, "I will make the letter M again." Write the letter. Then, "What is the name of this letter, John?"

You may also use the chalkboard to illustrate the likenesses in shape among the letters:

1. O, Q, C, G.
2. D, P, B.
3. N, M.
4. X, Y.

When the children have achieved some efficiency in identifying letters, you may introduce a game which will serve as a practice activity. Take sheets of plain newsprint paper (6 x 9 inches, for example,) and write a different letter on each sheet. (The letters are drawn at least 2 inches in height.) The sheets are passed out to the pupils, but not in alphabetical order. Then ask for the letters from the students. For example, "Who has the letter A ?" The student with the letter A stands and tacks the letter onto the bulletin board or wherever you wish to have the letters placed. The game continues until all the letters have been mounted.†

*The children should have no particular difficulty in making the adjustment from capitals to the lower-case letters they will encounter in reading. Most capital letters are the same as, or similar to, lower-case letters; six letters are distinctly different *(a, b, d, g, n, r)*.

†When you call for a letter, if the student with it doesn't respond, you can say, "The letter — is missing. I wonder where it is. Does anyone have the letter —? It looks like this." Write it on the board.

IDENTIFYING THEIR NAMES

Teaching the children to identify their own names should present no special difficulties. You will make use of the chalkboard in this manner: write a student's name on the board (in capital letters); while pointing to the first and last name, say, "John, this is your name — John Morgan." Have him come to the board and do the same, pointing to his first and last name and saying each.

"Now, you and I together will write your name." Have the student hold the chalk and, while you guide his hand, *slowly* write his name directly underneath. Write it together several times.

When this has been done with each student, erase the board and write a student's name on the board. "Will the student with this name come to the board?" Have the student stand by his name. Continue with the other students in the same way.

Also, you can make name plates for each student. They can be made of any suitable material, oak tag, for example. The name plates are taped to the childrens' desks. They may also be made for their personal possessions such as lunch boxes and notebooks.

This latter activity can be extended to the labelling of objects in the classroom. Use the unlined back of 3 by 5 file cards or cut writing paper to approximately that size. Print the words on the cards and tape them to the objects. *Use a single piece of tape for each card.* Many objects can thus be labelled in the classroom, including *door, desk, chair, closet, window, books, chalkboard, wall,* and *table.*

Regularly have the children review the name of the objects labelled by pointing to a label and asking, "What does this word tell us?" On another day, before the children come in, remove all the labels. Then pass out the labels giving one to each child. Ask each child to place his label on the appropriate object.

READING SIGNS

In some schools reading signs is part of the curriculum. When educators refer to a reading program for severely retarded children, they are apt to mean the children are taught to read signs for their safety and welfare and that is usually the extent of the "reading program."

There is an interesting paradox here. The prevailing point of view among educators is that the children have too little reading ability to be worth bothering about; yet, these same educators seriously make up lists of signs that include such words as *toilet, escape, station, poison, private, railroad crossing, hospital zone, admittance, entrance,* and *fragile.*

The writer has compiled and appropriately grouped a list of signs that are likely to be pertinent to the childrens' lives. Since it is impossible to compile a list of signs that would include different local conditions (for example, a farming area would have its own important signs), the teacher is invited to add to the following list:

Stay Away Signs	*Wait Signs*	*Toilet Signs*
keep out	stop	toilet
danger	do not walk	rest room
caution		men
closed	*In and Out Signs*	women
private		ladies
no trespassing	in	boys
no admittance	out	girls
men at work	enter	
poison	entrance	
wet paint	exit	
thin ice	push	
railroad crossing	pull	

Each group of signs can be printed on a large separate piece of oak tag. Draw a box around each word.

Stay Away Signs

Keep Out

Danger

etc.

The groups of signs can then be mounted on a classroom wall. They should be reviewed regularly (perhaps one group per lesson). Of course, you should explain the meaning of such words as *poison, wet paint,* and *railroad crossing.*

The following is a suggested practice activity which can be presented as a game. Ask the class to stand. Hold a stack of signs. (They can be made of oak tag.) Call on individual students to identify the signs. If a student gives the wrong answer, he must take his seat. The game continues until there is one student left standing, and he is the winner. You can introduce a little suspense towards the end of the game when there are only a few students standing by asking, "I wonder who the winner will be? Will it be Ed? Will it be Lois?"

SIGHT READING

It is important that the children develop a basic sight reading vocabulary. Without this, reading basal readers will be an uphill struggle.

The beginning writing vocabulary list on page 47 may serve as a beginning sight reading vocabulary list. The words on the list are basic in that a number of the words represent concepts that are relevant and important to the severely retarded child's life; the list also includes words commonly used in basal readers.

In teaching sight words, the teacher will utilize many variations. It is appropriate at this point to comment on elaboration, the importance of which has been presented by Kephart and others. If we were to hear only the theme of a Mozart, Bach or Beethoven composition repeated again and again, we would shortly become bored. What sustains and captivates our interest is the theme's elaboration — the series of variations that "spring" from the originally stated theme. While it is the theme itself that the composer wishes us "to learn," he impresses it upon us through multi-voiced variations and elaborations. Elaboration makes the theme (the basic concept) meaningful for listeners. The same is true of teaching. A basic concept becomes reality for students through a variety of related activities.

The following are some suggested variations on teaching sight words; write a number of words from the sight vocabulary on the chalkboard and circle the words for greater distinction:

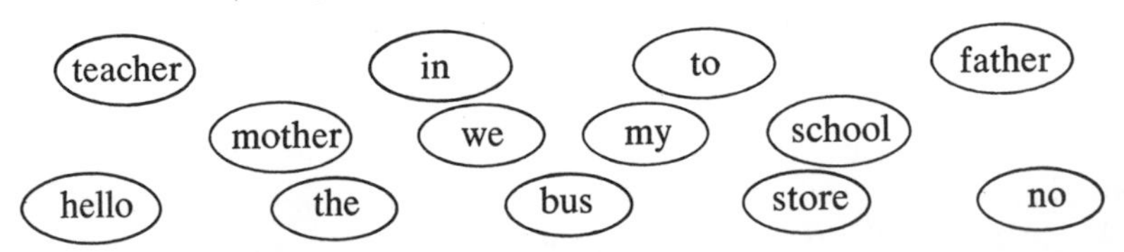

call individual students to the front of the room, then ask the students to find a word. For example, "Michael, can you find the word *mother*?"

Later, the student who has found the most words can act as the teacher; he will select words for other students to find. You may want to devise variations of the game, "Find the Word."

Another effective way of teaching the children sight words is to have them write the words. The procedure is as follows: write a series of words from the sight vocabulary list on the chalkboard; identify each word and have the children repeat each word after you; then call on individual students to read the words, not in the order they were first read, but backwards or skipping from one word to another; finally, have the children copy the words in their notebooks.

You can also use flash cards. The cards are made of oak tag with the words printed in large letters. Hold the stack of cards and simply "show" the foremost card to the class, asking the students to identify the word; then flick the card to one side or behind the stack, thus "flashing" the next word.

A BASIC UNDERSTANDING OF LETTER SOUNDS

Once the students have acquired a basic sight vocabulary of at least 30 words, they may be ready for the more demanding study of letter sounds. A basic sight vocabulary is a major step towards learning phonic skills; it provides severely retarded children with a "fund of words," plus needed self-confidence. Whether formally taught or informally learned (the latter seems to be true with many mentally normal), the acquisition of phonic skills, the writer believes, is indispensable to significant progress in reading.

The basic sight words the students have already learned can be used to illustrate letter sounds. The following list is based on the words of the beginning writing list on page 47; therefore, it is necessarily limited. However, this list may serve as a means of starting phonic instruction which may be continued by the teacher.

It is suggested that the teacher start the children on the consonant sounds and the combinations of consonant sounds indicated before having them go to vowel sounds. Because of the greater visual and auditory demands involved in phonics, it is also suggested that, in the beginning, the words used to teach letter sounds be short, preferably containing only two sounds (b-us, b-oy, c-ar, c-at) that letter sounds be initial consonants, and, whenever possible, initial vowels (side, egg).

(b) *b*us	(h) *h*ouse	(s) *s*leep
(c) *c*ar	(l) *l*ike	(st) *st*op
(d) *d*og	(m) *m*y	(th) *th*e
(f) *f*ather	(n) *n*o	(t) *t*oy
(g) *g*o	(p) *p*lay	(w) *w*e
	(r) *r*ide	(wh) *wh*ere*

(Pointing to the first letter in the word *bus*), "This letter tells us the sound is 'b'. Let's all say the sound." Then, as you point to the letter, call on individual students to make the sound. "What other words begin with the sound 'b'?" If the class response is poor, encourage discussion by saying, "I will say some words and when you hear the sound 'b' (repeat the sound several times), raise your hand. Now, listen carefully. *Tom is a boy*. Did you hear the sound 'b'? Listen again." When the students have identified the word *boy,* write it on the board, underneath the word *bus*. "What other words begin with the sound 'b', etc.?"

Cover only one letter sound in a lesson. When the students have studied the consonant sounds (of course, there should be regular reviews), present the vowel sounds in the same manner, stressing the following sounds: long *a,* pl*a*y; short *e,* h*e*llo; long *i,* r*i*de; and long *o,* g*o*.

Phonics is not an isolated study; it should be an integral part of the reading lesson. When students have difficulty with a word, encourage them to "sound" the word. "What is the first sound of the word?" The aim is the development of an independent method of word attack.

LEFT TO RIGHT SEQUENCE AND READING PHRASES

Teaching the students left to right sequence and the reading of phrases must necessarily be given together. However, to start, you can make the children aware of the left to right character of books.

Pass out any primer level texts which have both pictures and text. Then, go through the book page by page, with the students following in their copies. Point out the different pictures and discuss them with the children; emphasize the left to right sequence in pictures and text.

Provided the children have achieved some mastery of sight words, you can introduce phrases. At this point, you will have ample opportunities for pointing out the left to right sequence in reading. For example: write a series of phrases on the chalkboard; then read the phrases, and as you point to each word, exaggerate the left to right sequence with a large sweep

*When writing a word that contains a letter sound on the chalkboard, emphasize the appropriate letter(s) by making it darker than the other letters in the word—perhaps by using the side of the chalk or colored chalk.

of your arm.* The phrases, of course, will include only those words the children have already learned. Although there is a list of phrases on page 49, some typical ones are:

my toy	hello Mother
my dog	hello Father
the car	mother and father

You will find that the children have a tendency to read single word units rather than phrases. This is a natural tendency of all children, and you may meet this problem in two ways:

1. Stress the rhythmic flow of words. You can write the following phrases on the chalkboard, stressing the rhythmic accents as indicated:

   móther and fáther
   helló Móther
   helló Fáther

2. Stress the relationship between the spoken and written word. The children should be guided to the understanding that writing is another way of "saying." A writer cannot speak to all of us, so he does the next best thing—he speaks to us through his writing. In reading, whether it be phrases or stories, you will set the example, so read as though you are conversing and encourage the children to read phrases *as naturally as they would speak them.*

In writing, we are *conveying* our thoughts to others; in reading, we are *receiving* the thoughts of others. Thus, writing and reading are on the same continuum—they represent, respectively, the beginning and end of graphic communication. "In fact, the idea that through the reading of a series of words the complex thoughts of others might be communicated to us, was to be for my children one of the beautiful conquests of the future, a new source of surprise and joy."† Unless the children are guided to this discovery, reading will be merely a game—an interesting game, at best.

When the children have learned to identify most of the words in the beginning sight reading vocabulary list, they may be introduced to sentences and paragraphs. There are lists of sentences and paragraphs on

---

*When the children have acquired sufficient skill in reading consecutively from left to right, the teacher can simply point to the first word of a phrase.

†Maria Montessori, *The Montessori Method* (New York: Schocken Books, 1964), p. 304.

pages 49-50. You will find that two or three sentences or one paragraph is more than enough work for the children per lesson.

READING WITH FEELING AND UNDERSTANDING

There is a pressing need for special reading material for severely retarded children, since, to date, there is very little available in this field. The teacher, therefore, must frequently adapt materials. But, she faces the additional problem of finding those rare books that are both easy and interesting enough for the children to read. Too often a book is either easy enough but too childish, or it is mature enough but too difficult. Seldom do the twain—interest and readability—meet.

Because there are no special beginning reading series for severely retarded children, the teacher generally has no choice but to use a regular beginning series. Unfortunately, among the widely used basal series there are common deficiencies in terms of their appropriateness for severely retarded children. One such deficiency is their abstractness. Generally included in the vocabulary of pre-primer readers are such words as *help, here, something, do, it, make, down, up*. Severely retarded children are capable of learning such abstract concepts, but their presence in pre-primers makes beginning reading unnecessarily difficult.

Another deficiency of basic readers is that they seldom include real stories. Too often the stories are only tiny "slices of life," with little or no dramatic appeal. In stories for children, dramatic appeal derives from a main character's involvement with a *concrete* problem. Interest is sustained by the main character's attempt to resolve his problem. These elements are seldom found in beginning readers. Until such time as writers and publishers discover the severely retarded child with his particular needs for concrete language and strong story interest, he will have to read the tepid stories of regular basic readers.

Whatever reader is used, reading should be regularly assigned as homework. Therefore, a parent or someone else at home must help the child with his reading assignment; without this home practice it will be difficult for the child to progress in reading. A meeting with parents should be arranged, and a frank presentation should be made of the importance of the parents' role in developing a child's reading ability. Stress the necessity for cooperation between teacher and parents—what the teacher has done in the classroom is reinforced through practice at home. Such practice cannot always be done in class because there are other areas of the curriculum that have to be covered in a school day. Parents need not spend more than twenty minutes (certainly no more than half an hour) on an assignment. The teacher might illustrate a home reading assignment. "Now, let's say that John comes home with an assignment to read pages 4 and 5 of his pre-primer. In a quiet area of the house, sit by him and have him read to you; help him with words that he finds difficult; assist and encourage him. That's all you have to do."

The teacher very likely will find that parents are most willing to cooperate with her on this mutual task. They naturally want their children to read, but schools seldom have been willing to teach this skill. Frustrated by this unwillingness on the part of schools, parents have attempted this task alone, and with patience and determination, some have helped their severely retarded children achieve a modest, but gratifying, level of reading. With parental cooperation, home reading can be regularly assigned. In the beginning, one or two pages will be sufficient, but later, the children may be assigned a complete story.

A part of the reading lesson will be devoted to reviewing the home reading assignment. This cannot be done on a class basis since children progress at different paces and each child will be on a different page of his pre-primer. In the beginning, the teacher may go about the room having each student in turn read to her, or she may call the students, one at a time, to her desk to hear them read. When the students have achieved some facility in reading from pre-primers, the teacher may have individual students read to the class. This activity will offer the teacher opportunities to stress reading with feeling and understanding; it is also an excellent means of motivation. Reading to the class may be introduced in a manner similar to the following.

A student comes to the front of the room with his pre-primer and opens his book to the first page of a story (preferably one that he had for his last reading assignment). He holds up his book so that the class can see the beginning page. Ask the student to identify each person (or thing), the place, and what action is occurring in the picture. Then ask the student, "What is Jane saying?" The student responds by reading from the text. (Many basal readers do not include description or narrative in the text, but only the speech of characters.)

Remarks that are pertinent to a story are made to focus the children's attention on the action of the story and to heighten the suspense. You may do this while the student turns a page. "I wonder what Mary is doing." "I wonder what Mother is bringing." "Oh, I hope Tim can find his toy." Questions are an important technique in pointing out the continuity, meaning, drama and emotional nuance of a story.

STUDENT: "Little Rabbit saw something."
TEACHER: *I wonder what Little Rabbit saw?*
STUDENT: "She saw a hole."
TEACHER: *I wonder what kind of a hole it is?*
STUDENT: "A little brown hole!"
TEACHER: *I wonder what Little Rabbit did?*
STUDENT: "Down, down she went."
TEACHER: *Can you imagine Alice and Jerry's surprise?*
STUDENT: " 'Oh!' " said Alice and Jerry.*

A teacher cannot expect her children to read with feeling if she herself shows little feeling while reading. She must read in a whisper, with force, with a tremor in her voice; she must ask questions with a tight edge to her voice, with a lilt of excitement or with a note of sadness. In short, she must be an actress. Above all, the teacher should make a continuing effort to avoid having her children read in a monotone. She must stress that merely reading words correctly is not enough, the words must be read with feeling and understanding.

The children will respond positively in this direction for they enjoy reading. *Alice, Jerry, Dick, Jane* and other characters in the basic readers are like real people to them. A strong desire to read is characteristic of severely retarded children. This is understandable, for reading is a skill they associate with normally intelligent youngsters. When they are given basic readers and begin exploring the fascinating world of books, they feel they are not really so different from other children. The teacher should encourage this interest and identification. ("What does Jerry see?" "I wonder what Alice found?") The children should learn that books offer excitement, suspense and surprise.

The children's willingness to learn reading is half of "the battle." According to a widely used teacher's manual, "If a child is genuinely interested, he may learn to read with very little guidance."† The writer's experience bears this out. The children in the writer's class who learned to read basic readers seemed to find the right way themselves.

---

*Mabel O'Donnell, *The New Day In and Day Out: Basic Primer:* (Evanston, Illinois: Row, Peterson and Co.),p. 9.

†Ginn Basic Readers, *Manual for Teaching the Reading Readiness Program,* Part 1 (Boston, Mass.: Ginn & Co., 1961), p. 10.

chapter 3

Writing

What skills should the children be taught in writing? They should learn how to hold a pencil and pencil control, to write the alphabet and their names, and to write phrases, sentences, paragraphs, and simple letters.

Just as there are no easy formulas for teaching the fundamentals of writing to normally intelligent children, likewise, there are no easy formulas for teaching basic writing skills to severely retarded children. Although techniques outlined in this chapter have been used by the writer with enough success to justify their inclusion here, more effective methods of teaching writing skills to the severely retarded need to be developed, and teachers, of course, should be instrumental in developing and testing them.

HOLDING A PENCIL

The teacher may find that some of her children already have learned to hold a pencil properly. They may have learned this from a parent or on their own. Some children, who do not possess this ability, may be ready to acquire it without much difficulty; others, with insufficient finer motor coordination, will need to "work up" to this ability through such activities as art. Brush and crayon work afford the children practice in gripping a pencil-like object. Also, children like to draw on the chalkboard, and the teacher should encourage this by giving them a section of the board for their own use. Such activities help develop pencil control.

PENCIL CONTROL

An important technique for developing pencil control is the "filling-in" in crayon of outlined figures like those found in basic coloring books. At first the children will have difficulty staying within the outlines, but gradually they will learn to control the strokes of their crayons. Tracing is another technique for developing pencil control. Many classes for severely retarded children have geometric insets and inlay puzzles which can be used by the children for tracing. The pieces are held down firmly with one hand as the other traces with pencil their outline onto paper. The children can also trace figures in coloring books or pictures in magazines on onion-skin paper.

In addition, the children can learn to make straight lines. (Making a straight line is a major achievement for a severely retarded child.) Of the various straight lines, the vertical, perhaps, is the easiest to draw. The following are suggested exercises for teaching the children to draw vertical lines:

1. Draw a series of dots either on the chalkboard or on the children's papers:

   • • • •
   • • • •
   • • • •
   • • • •
   • • • •

   Trace a few series of dots—drawing the lines from the top downwards—to show the children how it is done. Then have the children do it.
2. Draw on the chalkboard Figure 3-1.

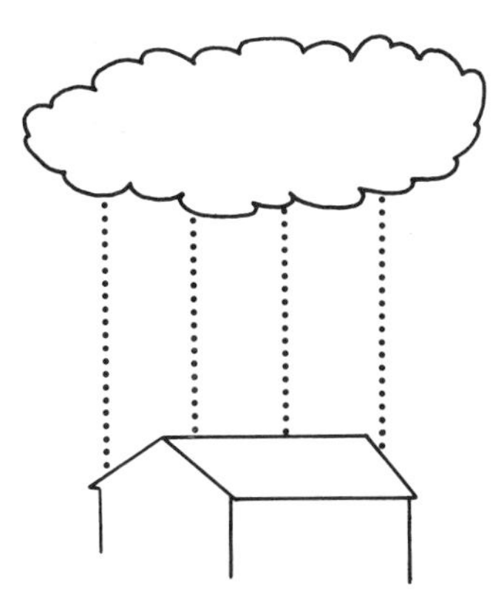

FIGURE 3-1.

Tell the class, "It is raining. We will trace the dots to show how the rain falls".

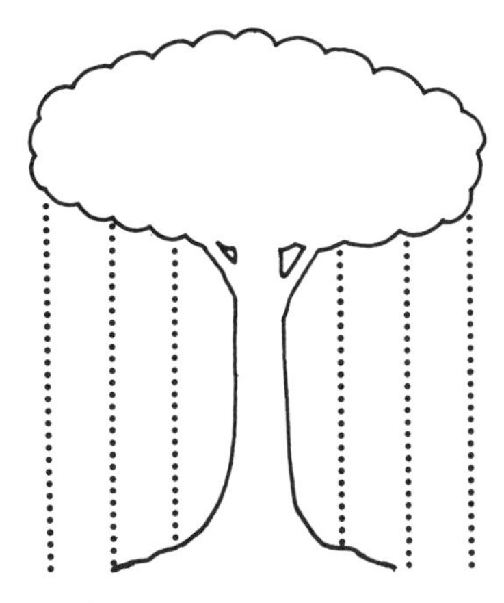

Tell the class: "When winter comes, leaves fall from the trees. We'll trace the dots to show how the leaves fall."

3. Draw a series of vertical lines on one line of lined paper. Then have the child draw a series of lines underneath.
4. Draw a series of vertical lines on the chalkboard. The lines should be drawn about four inches high. Each line is drawn slowly, emphasizing the straight downward stroke. Then have the children copy the lines in their notebooks.

Following the vertical line, which may take several weeks of instruction, the teacher may introduce the horizontal line.* At first this line should be presented alone, and later it may be related to the vertical line. Thus, in learning the horizontal line, the children will also be learning to form the letters T, L, H, F, and E (in that suggested order). Since the aim is pencil control, teaching the names of the letters at this time would be confusing to the children. Simply tell the children, "Let's put the two kinds of lines together like this." There are some subtle differences of line in certain letters which, in the beginning, are difficult for the children to form. For example, the letter E. The children will probably write this letter with each horizontal line the same length E. Letters that are less than perfectly formed are acceptable at this point.

In teaching the drawing of the horizontal line, the same procedure may be followed as with the vertical line, using the following stick figures:

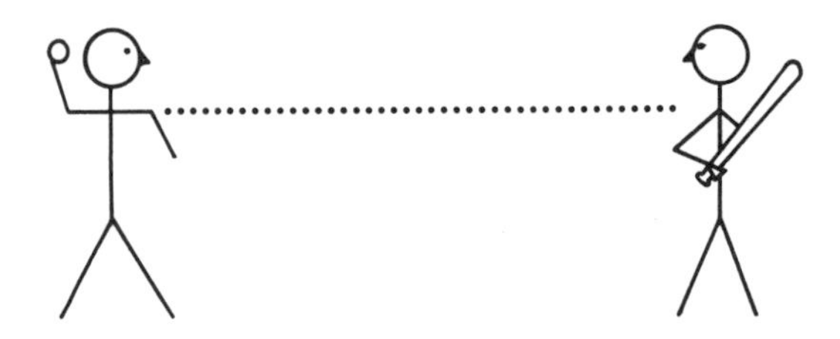

FIGURE 3-3.

Tell the class, "The drawing shows two boys playing baseball. We're going to throw the ball by tracing the dots. Who will be the first to throw the ball?"

FIGURE 3-4.

*The teacher may find it desirable to use terms other than "vertical" and "horizontal." For example: "line down" and "line across."

"This boy (girl) is bowling. The ball will follow the dots and hit the pins. Who will come to the board and hit the pins?"

Following the horizontal line, the teacher may introduce the curve. Again, this line should be presented alone, then related to another line. Thus, in learning the curve, the children will also be learning to form the letters **D**, **P** and **B** (in that suggested order). In teaching the curve, the following exercise and other figures devised by the teacher may be presented:

FIGURE 3-5.

"We're going to throw the basketball into the basket. Who will be the first to try to get it into the basket?"

FIGURE 3-6.

"The elephant wants to get the peanut. Who will help him get it?"

Following the curve, diagonal* lines may be introduced, first alone, then in relationship to other lines as they form the letters Y, X, V, M and N (in that suggested order). The following exercises and their variations may be used to help students draw the diagonal line:

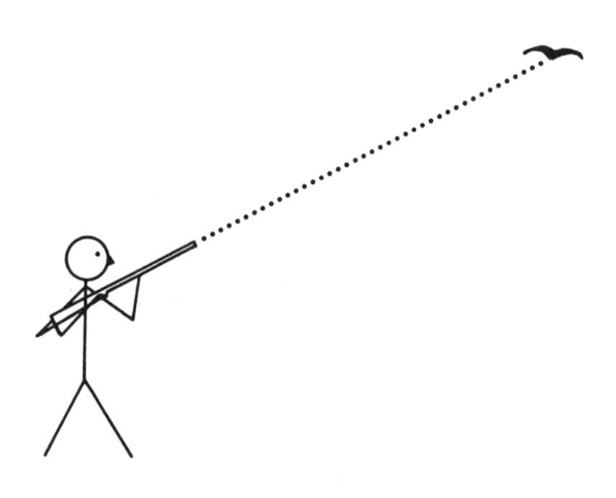

FIGURE 3-7.

"The hunter is shooting at the bird. Will he hit it?"

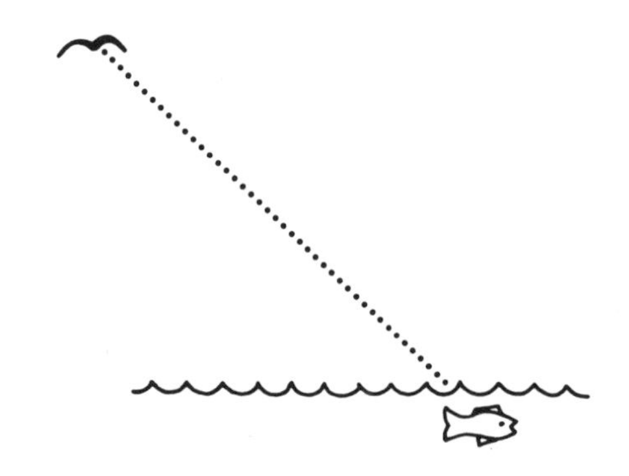

FIGURE 3-8.

"The eagle sees the fish in the water. Will he get it?"

*Instead of "diagonal," "slanting" or "leaning."

The purpose in teaching the children to draw vertical, horizontal, curved, and diagonal lines is to develop pencil control. The children will utilize their ability to draw and combine these lines when they begin a formal study of the alphabet.

THE ALPHABET

When they have mastered the drawing of vertical, horizontal, curved, and diagonal lines, the children have the ability to form the component parts of all the letters of the alphabet. If they have learned to combine the lines, they are ready to learn how to write the alphabet.

Upper case A has three component parts—two diagonal lines and one horizontal line / \ — (upper case letters are taught first since their configurations are simpler than lower case letters). The letter A, then, is made with three lines or strokes: / Λ A. A list of the letters with their components follows:

B I ᵓ ɔ. I I P I ᵓ

C C J I ˬ Q ( ) ˎ

D I ɔ K I ˊ ˎ R I ᵓ ˎ

E I ¯ - _ L I _ S ᶜ ɔ

F I ¯ - M / \ Λ Λ T I ¯

G C - N I I \ U I I ˬ

H I I - O ( ) V \ /

W V V Y (ˋ

X \ / Z / ¯ _

Note that letters O, Q and S are formed by combining two curved lines. For the children to form a circle in one stroke is more difficult than it is to do it in two strokes. This also applies to the letter S; it is easier to form this letter in two strokes than in one. When the children have acquired sufficient skill in writing letters this way, forming the letters O and S in single strokes will be comparatively easy.

In teaching students to write letters according to their component parts, it should be helpful to associate the configurations of the letters with familiar objects; thus, the children will not be faced with the task of making abstract strokes. The following list may be suggestive:

The letter A has a tent: Λ
The letter B has a flagpole: I
The letter C is like a half-moon: C
The letter D has a flagpole: I
The letter E has a flagpole: I
The letter F has a flagpole: I
The letter G has a half-moon: C
The letter H has two flagpoles: I I
The letter I has one flagpole: I
The letter J has a flagpole: I ; and it has a cup: ᴗ
The letter K has a flagpole: I
The letter L has a flagpole: I ; and it has a floor: _
The letter M has two flagpoles: I I
The letter N has two flagpoles: I I
The letter O is like a full moon: O
The letter P has a flagpole: I
The letter Q has a full moon: O
The letter R has a flagpole: I
The letter S is like a winding road: S
The letter T has a flagpole: I ; and it has a roof: ‾
The letter U has two flagpoles: I I ; and it has a cup: ᴗ
The letter V is like two fingers (middle and index):
The letter W is like two "V's" touching:
The letter X is like two crossed pencils (demonstrate)
The letter Y is like a tree: Y
The letter Z has a roof and a floor: ‾ _

Since the figures given are intended to be suggestive, the teacher can make any substitutions she wishes. For example, she may choose to call the two diagonals in the letter A a roof instead of a tent.

In forming letters, the children should work on lined paper. Since many lines may be confusing to them, it is recommended that they use unlined white paper with handdrawn sets of three lines. Thus, the letters of the alphabet would appear as shown on page 45.

If possible, the middle line should be made lighter than the other two lines. It would be even less confusing if only the top and bottom lines were used, but the middle line is a guide for A, B, E, F, G, H, J, K, M, P, R, W, X, and Y.

Raised-surface or textured-material letters, particularly sandpaper ones, are excellent for children who have difficulty learning the forms of letters. Using sandpaper letters mounted on smooth cards, the children lightly trace the letters with their index fingers in the same way they would write

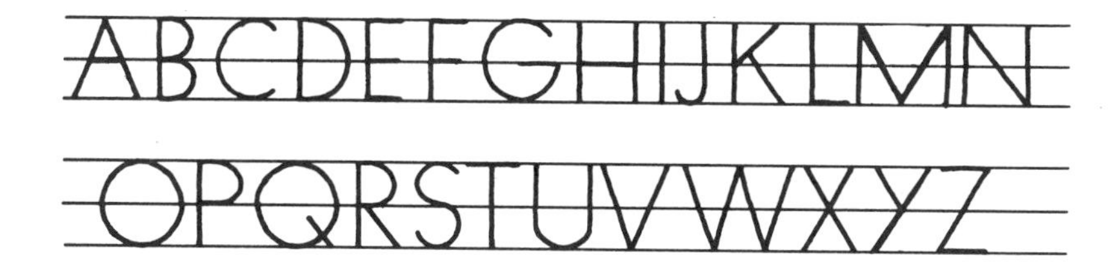

FIGURE 3-9.

the letters (supervised, in the beginning, to see that the letters are traced in the proper direction). This tactile-kinesthetic approach — pioneered and developed by Dr. Montessori—is a valuable aid for children to learn the form of letters.

Sandpaper, flock, beaded, and other raised-surface or textured letters can be purchased. Letters can be cut out of sandpaper or the teacher can simply write the letters on pieces of sandpaper with a crayon for the children to trace with their fingers.

WRITING THEIR NAMES

When the children have learned to form letters, writing their names should pose no major problems. However, the teacher should not expect the children to learn this skill in a few days; it may take weeks or months. The children should be given ample and varied opportunities for writing their names. For example:

1. At the beginning of each writing lesson in which the children will write in their notebooks, have them write their names at the top of the notebook page.
2. Have the children write their names on every written homework assignment they submit.
3. Have the children "sign" every piece of drawing and other art work they do.

4. When the children take out magazines or books from the school library, have them write their names on the library cards.

SPELLING

The writer has compiled a vocabulary list of 100 words. Many of the words were selected because of their concreteness and relevance; others were included to permit the writing of phrases and sentences. It is suggested that the teacher develop a beginning vocabulary list. The writer selected the first 30 words of the following list for his beginning vocabulary list. By using only these 30 words, whose presentation will be more than enough work for the children during one school year, the students were able to write phrases and sentences.

and	is	store
bus	like	teacher
car	love	the
dog	mother	this
father	my	to
go	play	today
hello	ride	toy
house	school	we
I	sleep	where
in	stop	work

a	children	he	saw
are	coat	her	see
at	desk	his	she
ball	dress	knife	sister
baseball	eat	look	sit
bed	eyes	night	sky
black	fast	on	star
blue	flower	pen	swim
boat	fork	pencil	table
book	friend	plane	train
boy	girl	pretty	tree
brother	grass	ran	walk
brown	green	read	water
cake	hair	red	went
can	has	roof	with
cat	hat	room	yellow
chair	have	run	your
		said	you

It is suggested that if the teacher uses the words of the above beginning vocabulary list, she introduce the words in the order of their concreteness. For example: *dog, bus, car, mother, father,* etc.

To begin, the children will simply copy the words. Write several words from the beginning list on the chalkboard. No more than two new words should be presented in a lesson. Make the letters three or four inches high, then have the children copy the words into their notebooks.

The children will need a great deal of practice copying the words before they will be able to spell them. Therefore, regular written homework assignments should be made to give students sufficient practice in writing the words. These assignments can be written in the children's notebooks (along with their reading assignments).

When the children have learned to copy the words, spelling exercises may be introduced. The following are suggested exercises:

Divide the chalkboard into three sections and select three students to go to the board. After assigning each of the students a section of the board, dictate several words and ask the students to write the words on the board. When all the words have been written, review the words by asking the students who did not go to the board, "Is this word correct? How do we spell it?" When the review is completed, you can count the number of correct words for each student: "Ed has spelled five words correctly. That's very good, Ed. John has spelled nine words correctly. That's great, John! Alan has spelled three words correctly. That's much better than yesterday, Alan."

Write a series of misspelled words on the board, then ask the students to give the correct spelling. For example, the following misspelled words are written on the board:

moter	(mother)	helo	(hello)
fater	(father)	techer	(teacher)
slep	(sleep)	schol	(school)
hose	(house)	lke	(like)
wrk	(work)	lov	(love)

Move down the list asking, "Is this the correct way to spell *mother?* How do we spell it? Is this the correct way to spell *father?* How do we spell it? *etc.*" For this exercise, utilize the misspelled words written by the students in previous lessons.

The children can also use movable letters. There is a wide variety of movable letters that are commercially available: cut-out cardboard letters, flannel board letters, magnetic board letters, plastic letters (for use with cork boards), plywood letters, interlocking metal letters, etc. Movable letters will give the children practice in spelling words from their writing vocabulary list and other words of their own (and the teacher's) choosing.

The children may be given spelling tests whenever the teacher thinks they are ready. The children are happy to have spelling tests since the tests give them a chance to "show what they can do." The tests, therefore, should be conducted in the same manner as those given to other youngsters. Each word is repeated, students are cautioned to keep their eyes on their own papers, the papers are graded, *etc.*

Spelling tests are important for several reasons. First, they serve a diagnostic purpose by showing where each child is in spelling. Second, spelling tests provide motivation; the children are encouraged to do their best. Third, such tests contribute to the children's self-esteem; this is evident in their enthusiasm to show the test papers to their parents.

PHRASES, SENTENCES, AND PARAGRAPHS

When the children have had extended practice writing words and made some progress in spelling, they may be introduced to phrases. The following suggested phrases are formed with only those words from the beginning vocabulary list:

my toy	hello Mother	the store
my dog	hello Father	the car
my house	hello Teacher	mother and father
my mother	the school	stop and go
my father	the bus	play and work
my teacher		

It is suggested that when the children are writing phrases, the teacher begin each writing lesson by asking, "What day is it today?" Then, when the day has been stated, the teacher writes at the top of the chalkboard—*Today is Monday*. The children copy this at the top of the page in their notebooks. The teacher may find that some of her children have difficulty copying words in sequence. They tend to copy one letter at a time and are apt to lose their place. This problem, of course, is caused by poor visual perceptual abilities—the inability to control the shift of focus of attention from the chalkboard to their paper, the inability to perceive the totality of the words they are copying, poor eye-motor coordination, etc. Perceptual-motor activities (presented in other books in Kephart's Slow Learner Series) given concomitantly with their academic work will help meet this problem. But, for the immediate task, it is suggested that the teacher write one word at a time on the chalkboard, instead of the whole phrase.

When the teacher thinks the children have achieved sufficient skill in writing, she may introduce sentences and paragraphs. The following sentences and paragraphs are formed by using only the words in the beginning vocabulary list:

Sentences

I play.	I love my father.
I sleep.	I love my mother.
I go to school.	This is my toy.
I like my teacher.	I like my toy.
I ride in the bus.	I like to play.
This is my house.	I like my dog.
My father works.	I like this car.

Paragraphs

Hello Mother. Where is Father.
Hello Father. Where is Mother.
We go to school. Hello teacher.
We go to my house. Hello Mother. Hello Father.
We go to school. In school we work and play.
This is my school. I like my school.
This is my house. My Mother is in the house.
This is my dog. I like my dog.
This is my toy. I like my toy.
I go in my house. Hello Mother. Where is my toy.
Where is the dog. The dog is in the house.
Where is Mother. Mother is in the house.
Where is the toy. The toy is in the house.
We go to school. We ride in the bus.
We go to the store. We ride in the car.
We ride to school in the bus. In school we work. In school we play.
I like school.

Commas, question marks, and other punctuation may be included, if the teacher wishes. It is suggested, however, that they be omitted at this point.

The teacher should not have the children write phrases, sentences, and paragraphs unless they can read them. Therefore, the teacher should have the children read the words on the chalkboard before they copy them. The teacher should not write words on the chalkboard without preliminary discussion, and the children should be guided to writing. "What new word did we learn this week? How do we spell it? Let's use the word in a sentence. Who can give me a sentence with the new word? Let's try to write that sentence. What is the first word of the sentence? How do we spell it?" The teacher then writes the first word of the sentence.

Also, the teacher may find that some of her children see little relationship between the written and spoken word; they tend to regard writing as merely a game-like activity. The teacher should stress that writing is another way of "saying." "When you go home each day, what is the first thing you say to your mother? 'Hello, Mother.' How do we spell *hello . . . Mother?"* (The teacher writes the phrase on the chalkboard.) "When we go home we say (pointing to phrase), 'Hello, Mother.' " Of course, the children will need regular practice in writing. It is unfair to the children to attempt to teach them any aspect of this complex skill without instruction at regular intervals.

WRITING LETTERS

The teacher should not introduce letter writing as an isolated activity, but should present it in relationship to immediate situations.

1. A child's older brother has recently entered military service. *"Wouldn't it be nice to write to your brother? He would be glad to hear from you."*
2. A thank-you note to the class mother for having the class to lunch in her home.
3. Get-well-soon letters from the class to one of the children who has been absent due to illness.

In the beginning, the teacher will have to write the letters for the children to copy. In most instances, she will use the chalkboard, but at other times, she will write the letters on paper for one or more students to copy. The teacher will not merely write a letter and then have the children copy it. She will encourage the children to contribute to the development of the letter. "What should we tell Mrs. Dowd? Well, didn't you have a good time at her home yesterday? Let's begin by telling her that."

Dear Mrs. Dowd,

We had a good time yesterday.

"What else should we say to Mrs. Dowd? Well, when someone does something nice, what do we say? We say thank you. Let's write that."

The teacher will point out the standard form of letters. The salutation: "Dear ________" (The comma after the salutation may be left out.) The closing: "Yours truly, love, *etc.*" In time the children will begin to write very brief letters without assistance. The following letter, written by Ed K. to his sister (after a year's instruction in writing), was *self-initiated and accomplished alone:*

Dear Joan,

I like school. We work and play.

Ed

chapter 4

one
two
three
four
five
six
seven
eight
nine
Sunday
Monday
Tuesday
Wednesday
Thursday
Friday
Saturday
Yesterday was

Arithmetic

What areas should be included in the study of arithmetic? The children should learn concepts of number, size, space, and time; counting; simple addition and subtraction; and the use of coins.* These areas have proved to be within the learning ability of some older severely retarded children. They may also be capable of learning such operations as simple multiplication and division. Therefore, the teacher need not consider the above areas of arithmetic as maximum goals.

NUMBER CONCEPTS

The following number concepts may be taught:

all	some
some	none
much	little
many	few
more	less

*The purpose of teaching the children addition and subtraction is to prepare them for handling coins effectively.

In teaching number concepts you can make use of such classroom materials as books, crayons, and pegs.

Write the word *many* on the chalkboard. (The word is written on the chalkboard to impress the students' memories with a visual concrete representation of the auditory word.) Then give examples of *many:* a stack of books, the contents of a large box of crayons, the contents of a box of pegs, *etc.* Next, write the word *few* on the chalkboard. Then, *using the same items used to illustrate many,* show *few* in comparison to *many* (e.g. place few pegs beside many pegs). Finally, using the above objects and other objects in the classroom, ask the students to identify *many* and *few* (e.g., showing a handful of pegs, "Is this many pegs or few pegs?")

You also can use the chalkboard to teach number concepts. Again, using *many* and *few* as an example, the following (or other) figures are drawn on the chalkboard:

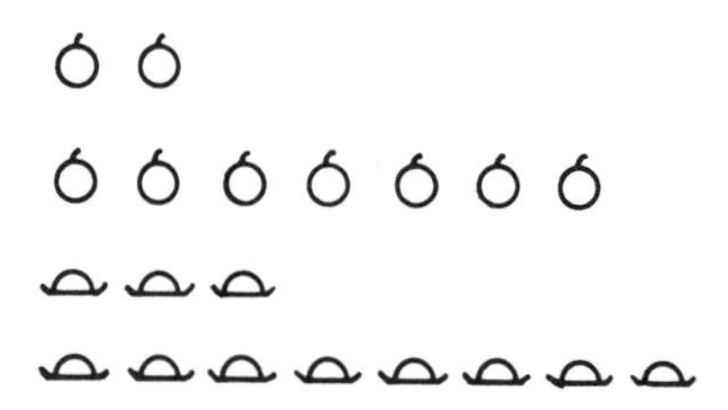

FIGURE 4-1.

First, identify the objects, "These are drawings of apples; these are drawings of hats." Then ask the following questions:

FIRST LINE: "Are these *few* or *many* apples?"*
SECOND LINE: "Are these *many* or *few* apples?"
THIRD LINE: "Are these *few* or *many* hats?"
FOURTH LINE: "Are these *many* or *few* hats?"

The teacher may find the Cuisenaire System valuable in arithmetical work with the children. The Cuisenaire System is a method of teaching arithmetic that utilizes colored rods of different lengths.† A Cuisenaire set consists of 241 rods,†† varying in length from approximately 3/8 of an inch to 4 inches (1 to 10 centimeters). The rods come in ten different

*Because children have a tendency to echo the latter part of a question, the correct answer should be stated first.

†In addition to rods, the Cuisenaire System utilizes charts and cards.

††Cuisenaire sets are now also available with 155 rods.

lengths and colors. Beginning with the smallest, the rods are white, red, light green, purple, yellow, dark green, black, brown, blue, and orange. Rods of the same color are of equal length; e.g., all white rods are the same length, all yellow rods are the same length, *etc.*

The essential process in the Cuisenaire System is the placing of rods end to end. Any of the rods may be placed end to end since all the rods have a cross-section of approximately 3/8 of an inch (1 sq. cm.). By manipulating the rods the children may learn various basic relationships: rods are of increasing or decreasing length; rods of the same color are equal; those of different colors are unequal; several rods placed end to end will equal a single larger rod (e.g., two white rods equal one red rod). Through the manipulation of the rods, more complex relationships such as multiplication, division, fractions, geometry, and algebra, may be taught.

The system was devised by a Belgian educator, Georges Cuisenaire. In 1952, Cuisenaire formally presented his method in a book, *Numbers in Colour*. Cuisenaire held that the traditional method of teaching arithmetic was inadequate. He believed that children could more effectively learn arithmetical relationships by manipulating and seeing the qualities of the material. Since 1952, the system has undergone further development, due mainly to the efforts of Dr. Caleb Gattegno, a former British educator now working in the United States with inner-city children.

In recent years there has been increasing interest shown in the Cuisenaire System. Some schools, particularly in Europe, have formally adopted the method in their arithmetic curriculums. In the United States, the system is being tried on an experimental basis by some school districts. In the Brentwood School District of Long Island, educators are experimenting with the Cuisenaire rods in kindergarten to fourth grade classes. Although the Cuisenaire System was devised for normally intelligent children, the writer has found it useful in teaching arithmetical relationships to severely retarded children. Its full potential for this group of children is yet to be determined.

The following activities are suggested for teaching number concepts with Cuisenaire rods:

ALL, SOME

Pass out the sets of Cuisenaire rods to the children (one set of rods for a group of two or three students).* Then say, "Look at *all* the rods (indicating with a motion of your hand). Now, I will take *some* from Edward, *some* from Jane, *some* from Bill, *etc.*"

---

*Sets may be purchased from the Cuisenaire Company of America, Inc., 12 Church Street, New Rochelle, N.Y. 10805.

Place a stack of rods before one student and say, "Joseph has *all* the rods. So I will take rods from Joseph and give *some* to Mary, *some* to Jim, *etc.*"

Indicate your desk and say, "I have no rods." Then go about the room, saying, "May I have *some* rods?" (Or, "Who will give me *some* rods?")

SOME, NONE

Place several rods in the open palm of your hand and say, "I have *some* rods." Then take the rods away and say, "Now I have *none*."

Place a few rods in one of your hands behind your back, then bring forth one hand. Students have to guess whether there are *some* rods in your hand or *none*. (This activity may be varied by having students, in turn, stand before the class and do the same thing.)

MANY, FEW

Place several rods before a student and say, "Mary has a *few* rods." Then move on to the next student and place many rods before him and say, "Mary has *few* rods, but look here, Charles has *many* rods." (This activity can be varied; for example, the rods can be placed in the palm of the student's hand instead of on his desk, or you can ask students to give *few* and *many* rods to each other.)

MORE, LESS

Place a number of rods before a student and several rods before another student, then say, "Alan has *more* rods than Johnny; Johnny has *less* rods than Alan." Reverse the number of rods. Then say, "Now, Johnny has *more* rods than Alan, and Alan has *less* rods than Johnny."

Place four or five small rods in a student's hand and two small rods in his other hand. "Which hand has *more* rods?" "Which hand has *less* rods?"

The following activity may be used as a review of number concepts:

After passing out the sets of rods to the students, say, "I have passed out *all* the rods to you, so I have *none* (indicating your desk). May I have *some* rods, Lois? (The rods are brought to your desk.) Now I have *some* rods. But I have *less* rods than you (the class). You each have *many* rods, but I have only a *few* rods. I would like to have as *many* as you. Who else will give me *some* rods? Ed is giving me *some* rods; Alan is giving me *some* rods; Susan is giving me *some* rods; *etc.* Oh, look! Now I have *more* rods than you."

SIZE CONCEPTS

The following size concepts may be taught:

big	little	largest	smallest
tall	short	long	short
taller	shorter	longer	shorter
tallest	shortest	longest	shortest
large	small	bigger	smaller
larger	smaller	biggest	smallest

In teaching concepts of size, as with number concepts, you can use classroom materials such as books, pencils or crayons. Any set of objects of different lengths can be used (two books, two pencils, *etc.*)

The concepts of *long* and *short* may be introduced using only two pencils. Identify the *long* pencil and the *short* pencil. Then ask the class to identify them, "Which is the *long* pencil? Which is the *short* pencil?" Next, reverse the position of the pencils and ask the class to identify them. "We'll do it again. Which is the *long* pencil? etc."

Teaching the comparative and superlative should pose no special problems. Simply phrase your description of the objects and your questions in the comparative or superlative sense, "Which is *longer*? Which is *shorter*? Which is *longest*? Which is *shortest*?"

You also can use the chalkboard to teach concepts of size. The following figures (or other figures) are drawn on the chalkboard:

FIGURE 4-2.

First, identify the figures, "These are drawings of houses, boats, and buses." Then ask the following questions:

1. a. "Is this a *big* or *little* house?"
   b. "Is this a *little* or *big* house?"

2. a. "Is this a *big* or *little* boat?"
   b. "Is this a *little* or *big* boat?"

3. a. "Is this a *big* or *little* bus?"
   b. "Is this a *little* or *big* bus?"

You may also use the Cuisenaire rods to teach concepts of size. Hold up the orange rod. "The orange rod is a *big* rod." Hold up a white rod. "The white rod is a *little* rod." Then hold up both rods. "Which is the *big* rod? Which is the *little* rod?" Of course, other rods may also be used. Hold up both the yellow rod and the red rod, "The yellow rod is *bigger* than the red rod. The red rod is *smaller* than the yellow rod." Then reverse the rods, "Which is the *bigger* rod? Which is the *smaller* rod?" The superlatives may be introduced in the same manner, except that three or more rods are used.

You may find that building stairs with the rods is helpful in developing concepts of size. Although children can use all ten sizes to build stairs, since the smaller-sized rods are easier for the children to manipulate, it is recommended that at first they use only the five smaller rods: the white, red, light green, purple, and yellow rods. The stairs may be built flat on the desks or perpendicular to it.

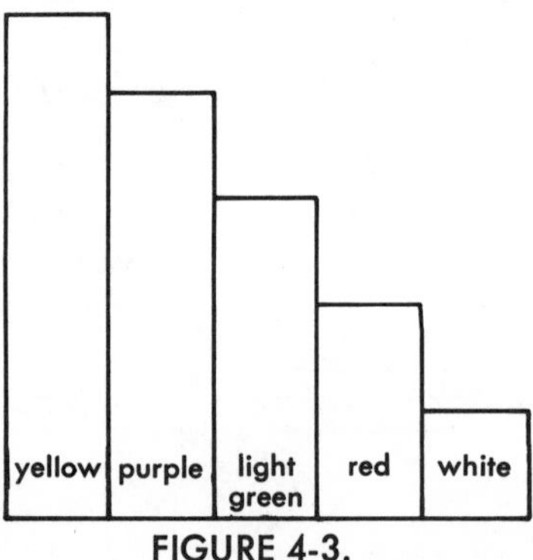

FIGURE 4-3.

The following are suggested activities using stairs:

Have children build stairs flat on their desks. Ask them to point to the *longest* rod (the orange, if they are using all ten sizes, the yellow, if they are using the first five sizes) and to the *shortest* rod (the white).

Have the children build stairs perpendicular to their desks. Ask them to point to the *tallest* rod and to the *shortest* rod.

Using the rods, the children can play a game. As a pupil holds both hands behind his back, place a different-sized rod in each hand. Then say, "Without looking, show me the *big* rod," (or, "Show me the *little* rod."). The concepts of *large* and *small*, *bigger* and *smaller*, and *larger* and *smaller* may be handled in the same manner.

Some suggested rod combinations for this game are:

white and yellow	yellow and purple
white and purple	purple and light green
white and red	light green and red

This game reinforces concepts of size because the children must depend on their tactile sense alone.

Be sure to have the children put away the Cuisenaire sets themselves. Having the children replace the rods in their proper compartments according to color and size is an excellent activity for developing perceptual abilities.

SPACE CONCEPTS

The following concepts of space may be taught:

high	low	behind	in front of
top	bottom	empty	full
over	under	left	right
up	down	above	underneath
in	out	between	
inside	outside	on	off
front	back	beginning	end

As with number and size concepts, space concepts may be taught using classroom materials. Place a chalkboard eraser on the top edge of the chalkboard and another eraser on the chalk tray, then say (pointing), "I placed this eraser *high*, and I placed this eraser *low*."

Another approach to teaching concepts of space is using the human body in action. Have the children play the game "Airplane." A student acts as the pilot; his hand is the airplane, and his desk is the airport. You are the control tower operator who gives instructions for taking-off, flying around the airport and landing, "Go *up*. Go *down*. Go *left*. Go *right*, etc." If you wish, all the students can be pilots at the same time (a little confusing, but fun for the children) while you give "control tower instructions," "Are you all ready for take-off? Okay, here we go. Up, up, up, etc." Use as many of the given concepts as you can.

Tell and show the class how the game "Simon Says" is played. Then say, "Simon says place hands *over* your head. Simon says place hands *under* the desk. Simon says place hands *over* your eyes. Simon says *right* hand up. Simon says *left* hand behind your back, *etc.*" Stand before your desk and say, "I am standing in *front* of my desk. . . . Now, I am standing in *back* of my desk. . . . Now, I am standing in *front of* Bill, and Bill is standing in *back of* (or *behind*) me. . . . Now, Bill is standing *in front of* me, and I am standing in *back* of (or *behind*) Bill, *etc.*" Ask a student to stand by you, then ask another student to stand *between* you and the first student. Ask student *A* to come to the *front* of the room, then ask student *B* to stand in *back* of student *A*, student *C* to stand in *back* of student *B*, and student *D* to stand in *back* of student *C*. Then, when the last student is in place, reverse the line and ask student *D* to stand in *front* of student *A*, student *C* to stand in *front* of student *D, etc.*

You also can use Cuisenaire rods to teach concepts of space. Take any two different sized rods, e.g., the orange and blue rods, and demonstrate the concepts of *top* and *bottom* using the two rods, "I put the blue rod on *top* of the orange rod. The orange rod is at the *bottom*." The pupils, at their desks, do likewise. Then ask, "Which rod is at the *top*? Which rod is at the *bottom*?" (The activity may be continued using different pairs of rods.)

Have the class build up a series of rods in this way: the orange rod is placed flat on their desks, and on top of it the children place the blue rod; then point out the bottom and top rods. "The orange rod is at the *bottom*, and the blue rod is on the *top*." Next, the brown rod is placed on top of the blue rod. "Now the brown rod is on *top*. Which rod is *between* the brown and orange rods? (the blue)" "Which rod is at the *bottom*? (the orange) Which rod is *on* the orange rod? (the blue) Which rod is *on* the blue rod? (the brown)" The class then places the next size rod, the black, on top, and the same kinds of questions are asked. The exercise may be continued until the ten rods in the set are placed.

TIME CONCEPTS

The following concepts of time may be taught:

night	day	days of week
next		months of year
before	after	seasons
early	late	telling time
fast	slow	

Teaching concepts of time is particularly challenging. Severely retarded children have very little conception of time. Perhaps at the heart of this problem is the weakness of their mental associations. Normally, certain activities are associated with different times of the day. Therefore, in teaching the concepts of *night* and *day,* point out through discussion that at night (when it is dark), they eat supper, watch television, get ready for bed, *etc.*; in the day (when it is light), they get up, get washed and dressed, eat breakfast, come to school, *etc.*

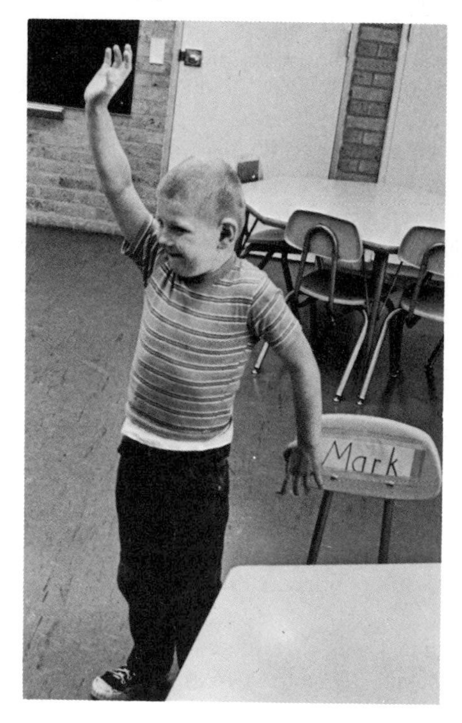

Before the children can learn to tell time on a clock, they must understand what a clock does. Telling the children that a clock measures time will be meaningless to them. You must *show* them the measuring of time. *(Time is movement: the never-ending sequence of events.)* Point to the clock in the classroom (it should be large enough for the children to see clearly the action of the large hand) and say, "A clock has two hands. A short hand (pointing to it) and a long hand (pointing to it). Today you are going to study the long hand. Now, watch the long hand and when you see it move, raise your hand. (The children, at first, will very likely respond with shouts of delight, instead of raising their hands.) Yes, some of you saw the large hand move. Now let's watch the large hand again. (This may be repeated several times.) Now, while you wait for the large hand to move again, I will take a walk. But you must keep your eyes on the large hand." Then slowly begin walking around the classroom and continue walking until the clock ticks off one minute. Then say, "Well, that was a nice walk I took while you looked at the clock. How long did my walk take? (Show them where the long hand was at first and where it moved.) The long hand moved once (hold up one finger). My walk took one minute." Then walk for two minutes as the children watch the long hand. "How long did that walk take?"

A variation of the above activity follows. "Now (today), I will do something else. Look at the clock." Improvising, take off your shoes, stretch and yawn, sit at your desk, then rest your head on the desk and pretend that you fall asleep. "Awaken" when the large hand has ticked off a minute. "How long was I asleep?" Individual students also can take walks and naps while the rest of the class watches the clock.*

The children should have comparatively little difficulty learning (memorizing) the days of the week, as charts 5 and 6 suggest.

COUNTING

How high can the children learn to count? It is difficult to say at the present time, since only a limited amount of information about the children's ability in counting is available. But, there is no doubt in the writer's mind that many of the children can learn to count to at least 20 with understanding.

It should be pointed out that there are two kinds of counting: rote counting, merely saying the names of the numbers, and true counting, counting with understanding. Of course, the aim is to have the children

*The preceding activities may also be used in studying the second hand on a clock.

CHART 5.

	Sept. 28	Oct. 7	Oct. 13	Nov. 1	Nov. 22	June 2
Alan P.	MTW	MTW	MTWThFSS	MTWThFSS	MTWThFSS	MTWThFSS
Ed K.	MTWThFSS	MTWThFSS	(Absent)	MTWThFSS	MTWThFSS	MTWThFSS
Alan G.	MTW	MTW	MTWThFSS	MTWThFSS	MTWThFSS	(Absent)
Irene S.	MTW	(Absent)	MTW	MTWThFSS	MTW-FSS	MTWThFSS
Thomas F.	MT	MTWTh	MTWTh	MTWThFS	MTWTh-SS	MTW-FSS

CHART 6.

	Oct. 13	Oct. 20	Nov. 1	Nov. 9	Nov. 22	Dec. 19
Alan P.	Jan.	Jan.-Aug.	Jan.-July	Jan.-Dec.	Jan.-Dec.	Jan.-Dec.
Ed K.	Jan.	Jan.-April	Jan.-Dec.	(Absent)	Jan.-Sept.	Jan.-Dec.
Alan G.	Jan.	Jan.-May	Jan.-Dec.	(Absent)	Jan.-Dec.	Jan.-Dec.
Irene S.	Jan.	(Absent)	Jan.-Sept.	Jan.-Dec.	Jan.-June	Jan.-Dec.
Thomas F.	Jan.	Jan.-	Jan.-March	Jan.-Dec.	Jan.-Sept.	Jan.-Dec.

attain skill in actual counting. But, rote counting has its value; by its use, the children can learn the labels or names of numbers.

Rote counting should pose no difficulty for the children. Certainly, it will be easier for them than actual counting.

It can be taught by various means. You can simply have the children recite the numbers, or you can provide them with a visual crutch, such as a series of apples (or any other figure), drawn on the chalkboard. Have the children repeat the names of the numbers as you count. Place a stack of books on your desk and count them with the students repeating the numbers after you.

It should be stressed that in the above exercises you are not teaching the essence of counting—quantitative relationships—but rather, giving the students something upon which to build a series of memorizations. Keep in mind that your aim is to teach the children to use, to read, and to write numbers.

The chalkboard is a useful aid in giving the children practice in reading and writing numbers. The following are suggested activities:

Write the numbers 1 to 10 and have the children copy the numbers in their notebooks, then identify each number for the children and have them repeat the names of the numbers. Next, call on individual students to read the numbers *both forward* and *backwards.*

Write the numbers 1 to 10 on the chalkboard in this manner:

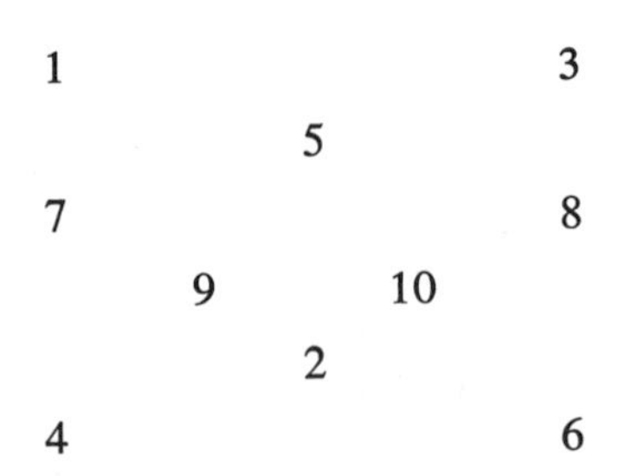

"Today we are going to play a game. The game is called 'Find a Number.' John, will you begin? Can you find number *5*? (Have the students come to the board and point to the number.) Mary, can you find number *4, etc?*"

Draw a house and a pond. On the pond, draw stepping stones, and on each stepping stone write a different number:

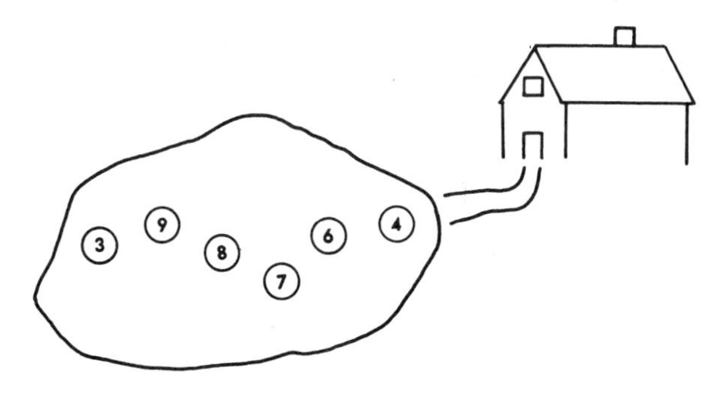

FIGURE 4-4.

"Today we are going to play another game. The game is called 'Going to Grandmother's House.' Here is a drawing of Grandmother's house. In front of her house is a pond. This is the pond. To cross the pond, you must walk on these stepping stones. You walk on the stones by reading the numbers. Now, let's begin. Steve, can you get to Grandmother's house?" The students should come to the board and point to each number as they say them. Change the numbers after a student has read them correctly.

Write a series of nonconsecutive numbers on the chalkboard:

1	2	3	6	5	4	7
8	9	12	11	10	1	2
4	3	5	6	8	7	9
10	12	11	1	16	10	8
7	4	7	9	12	11	5

Then call on individual students to read one line each.

A game can be played by having a student come to the board and write any series of numbers he chooses, then have the class read the numbers.

The chalkboard is helpful in teaching the children the use of numbers. Several illustrative exercises follow:*

Draw a series of apples on the chalkboard as shown in figure 4-5.

---

*The total series of figures may be confusing to the children. To simplify the exercise, draw each row of figures separately; when the students have identified the number of figures, erase them and draw the next series of figures.

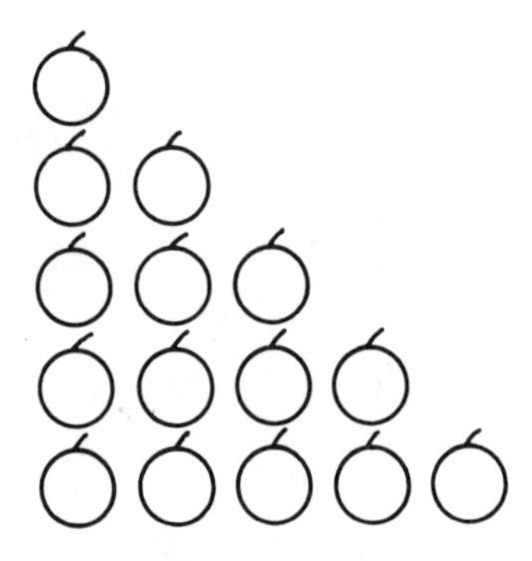

FIGURE 4-5.

"This is a drawing of one apple. How many apples are there on the next line? Let's find out. One, two; there are two apples on this line. How many apples are there on the next line? Let's find out. Count with me, *etc.*" As the number of apples on each line is stated, the appropriate number symbol is written:

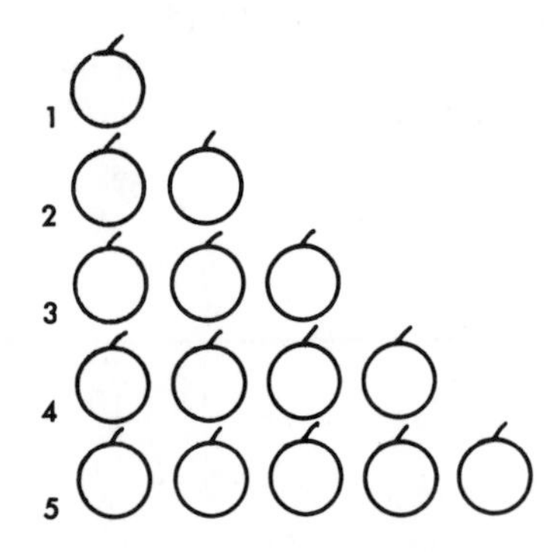

FIGURE 4-6.

The above exercises may be varied by using stick figures as shown in figure 4-7.

Classroom objects can be used to teach the use of numbers. Pass out stacks of books of varying numbers to the students, then have each student count the stack of books on his desk. Since their eye-hand coordination is poor, have them hold each book with both hands as they count. After they have counted their stack of books, have them exchange stacks and count these.

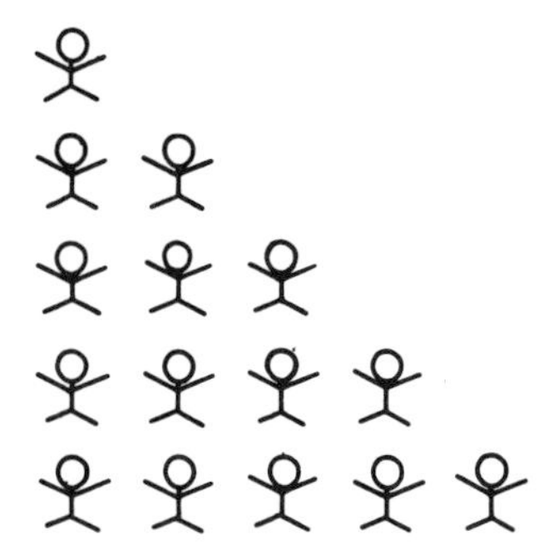

FIGURE 4-7.

You can also have individual students count the other children in the class. Have a student come to the front of the room and ask him to do the following:

a. Count the boys in the class
b. Count the girls in the class
c. Count all the students in the class

Because their perceptual manipulations are limited, have the students walk about the room, pointing to or touching each classmate as they count.

Have a student come to the front of the room. Ask the class a series of questions to which the students respond by raising their hands. You may ask such questions as, "How many of you have a brother or sister in this school?" "How many of you watch the ________ show on television?" "How many of you can swim?" As the students respond to each question, the student in front of the room counts the number of raised hands.

You also can have the children use practice books. There have been some excellent kindergarten number books published which provide the children with practice in reading, writing, and using the numbers 1 to 10.*

ADDITION AND SUBTRACTION

Teaching addition and subtraction in the traditional manner *(one plus one is two; two minus one is one)* to severely retarded children is a waste of time. The children merely mouth the formulas with no comprehension

*For example, see M. Ambrose, *Happy Ways to Numbers* (New York: Holt, Rinehart and Winston), 1967.

of the quantitative relationships involved. A different approach must be used, and the following suggested methods may prove useful.

Again, you will utilize the chalkboard. With a minimum of drawing ability, you can represent simple objects so that the children can *see* quantitative relationships.

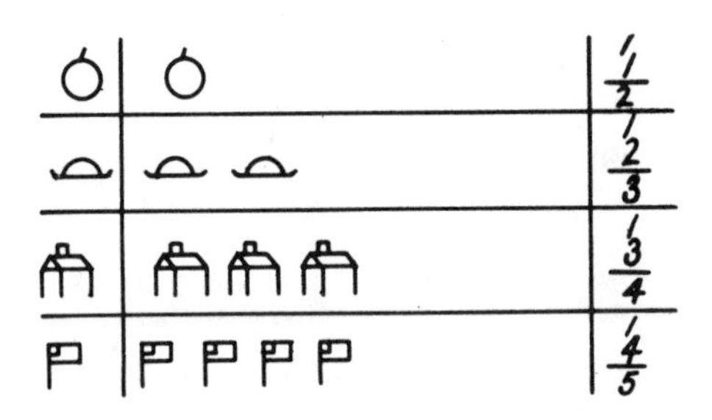

FIGURE 4-8.

First, identify each object, then say, "Here is one apple. Here is another apple. One apple and one apple are two apples. We write that in this way:

$$\begin{array}{r} 1 \\ \underline{1} \\ 2 \end{array}$$

Now, here is one hat, and here are two hats. One hat and two hats are three hats."

Classroom objects also can be used. Pass out books to the pupils. One book to student *A*, two books to student *B*, three books to student *C*, four books to student *D*, etc. "*A* has one book. How many books do you have, *B*? Yes, *B* has two books. Now, *A*, will you pick up *B*'s books? How many books do you have now, *A*? Yes, three books. One book and two books are three books. How many books do you have, *C*? Yes, *C* has three books. Now, *A*, will you pick up *C*'s books? How many books do you have now, *A*? Yes, six books. Three books and three books are six books. Now, how many books do you have, *D*, *etc.?*"

The children also can use coins. Have them use only one cent pieces in the beginning. Pass out one penny to each student. "How many pennies do you each have?" Pass out another penny to each student. "How many pennies do you have now?" Have each student give you back one penny. "Now, how many pennies do you have?" Pass out two pennies to each student. "How many pennies do you have now?" Have them each give you back one penny. "How many pennies do you have now?" Give out three pennies to each student, etc.

You should find Cuisenaire rods useful in teaching addition and subtraction. It is suggested that, in the beginning, the students work only with the five smallest rods: white, red, green, purple, and yellow. The rods are given the following values:

white	1
red	2
green	3
purple	4
yellow	5*

You may have the children begin by building stairs. The children place the yellow rod flat on their desks (the stairs may also be built perpendicular to their desks), then they line up the following rods in this order: purple, green, red, and white. Ask, "Who can go down the stairs?"† The children respond by reciting the above values as they point to each rod (5, 4, 3, 2, 1).

Next,‡ you may have the class work with one group of rods—green for example. The children place a single green rod on their desks. Tell them they are going to make a train. Ask them to place another green rod end to end with the first rod. Then (pointing) say, "How many rods do we have now? Yes, two rods. Let's add another green rod to our train. How many rods do we have now? Count them. Yes, three rods. Let's add another green rod to our train, *etc.*"

Subtraction can be introduced in this exercise, "How many rods do we have now? Yes, six rods (for example). Let's take away one rod from our train. How many rods do we have now? Yes, five rods. Let's take away another rod. How many rods do we have now? etc." At a later date, you may introduce the written symbols. As above, the students begin by making a train; then you say, "Now, we can show that one rod and one rod are two rods. Do you know how we can show it? Write:

$$\begin{array}{r} 1 \\ 1 \\ \hline 2 \end{array}$$

."

Another suggested activity with rods is to have the children take a red rod (which has the value of 2) and place a white rod on top of it:

---

*These values are not arbitrary since the white rod is the basic unit. Therefore, the red rod equals two white rods, the green rod equals three white rods, *etc.*

†Do not have the children go up the stairs (1, 2, 3, 4, 5) as they may confuse the counting of the rods for their numerical values.

‡Each exercise will be more than enough work for a lesson, though, of course, each exercise will have to be repeated a number of times.

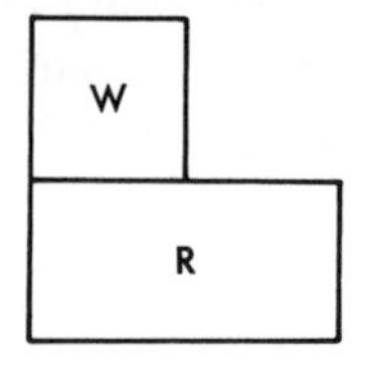

FIGURE 4-9.

Next, have the children place another white rod in the space beside the first white rod. "One white rod and another white rod equal a red rod; we can write that in this way: $\begin{array}{c}1\\1\\\hline 2\end{array}$." To make the quantitative relationships clearer, draw this on the chalkboard:

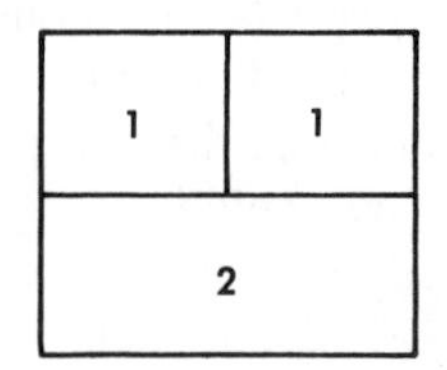

FIGURE 4-10.

It should be helpful to mark the numerical value on each rod (granted, a big task for the teacher), perhaps by taping the numbers on the rods.

Instruct the children to take a green rod (given the value of three) and on top of it to place a white rod:

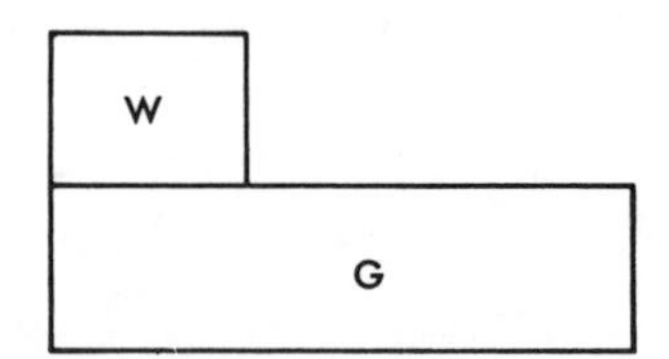

FIGURE 4-11.

The children are then asked to find a single rod that will fit in the space (beside the white rod). When the red rod has been placed next to the white rod, "A white rod and a red rod equal a green rod; we can write that in this way: $\begin{array}{c}1\\2\\\hline 3\end{array}$." In a similar manner, the children may continue with other rods: the purple rod (4), and above it a white rod (1) and a green rod (3), $(1 + 3 = 4)$; the yellow rod (5), and above it a red rod (2) and a green rod (3), $(2 + 3 = 5)$.

To introduce the concept of subtraction, the procedure is similar to that outlined above. Two white rods are placed end to end above a red rod, then one of the white rods is taken away. Thus, the children can see that when one white rod is taken away from atop the red rod, one white rod is left: two minus one is one. Later, the children may work with more combinations which equal a first rod.

The green rod and its combinations:

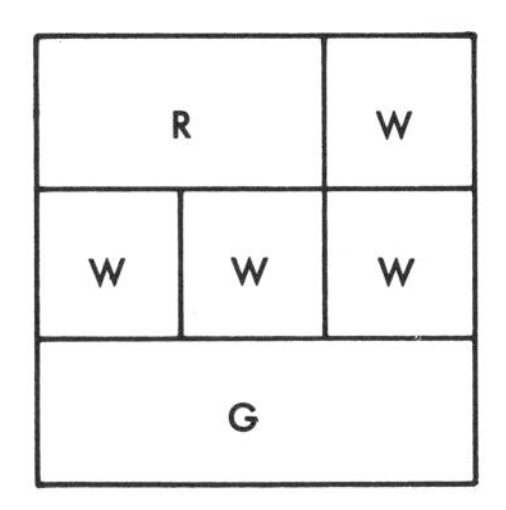

FIGURE 4-12.

Thus, the three white rods equal the green rod: $1 + 1 + 1 = 3$; the red rod and the white rod also equal the green rod: $2 + 1 = 3$.

The yellow rod and its combinations:

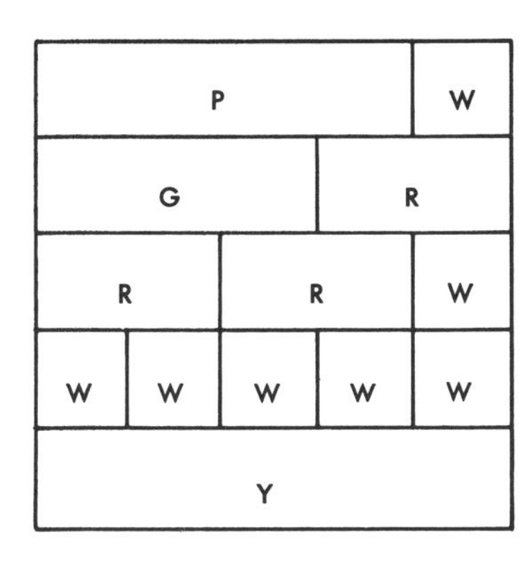

FIGURE 4-13.

The five white rods: $1 + 1 + 1 + 1 + 1 = 5$; the two red rods and the white rod: $2 + 2 + 1 = 5$; the green rod and the red rod: $3 + 2 = 5$; and the purple rod and the white rod: $4 + 1 = 5$; the preceding combinations all equal the yellow rod.

Subtraction is readily representable with combinations; for example, using the yellow rod and two of its combinations:

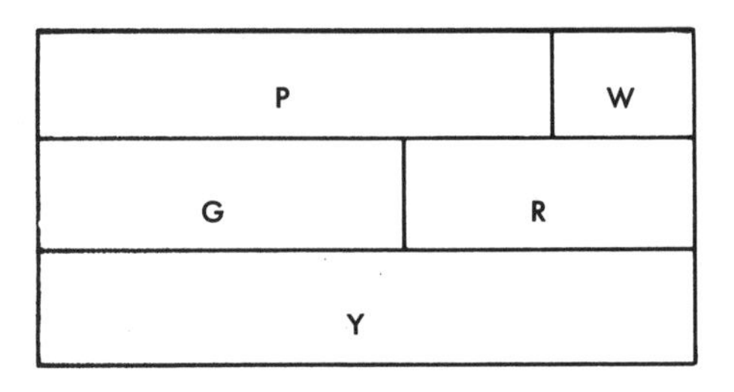

FIGURE 4-14.

With the yellow as 5, the purple as 4, the green as 3, the red as 2, and the white rod as 1, the children may see that if they take a white rod away from the top line, the purple rod is left; thus: $5 - 1 = 4$. Continuing, if the purple rod is taken away, the white rod is left; thus: $5 - 4 = 1$; if the red rod is taken away (second line), the green rod is left; thus: $5 - 2 = 3$; and if the green rod is taken away, the red rod is left; thus: $5 - 3 = 2$.

The writer believes there is a great potential for the effective teaching of arithmetical concepts to severely retarded children using Cuisenaire rods. Further development, refinement, and exploration are needed. The teacher, therefore, should go beyond this beginning.

HANDLING COINS

The teacher may well find that teaching the handling of coins is particularly challenging and interesting. There are many possibilities for extending the children's experience, understanding, and ability in this area. The teacher may have the children go on field trips to local stores. At first, the purpose may be merely to acquaint the children with the physical layout (the meat counter, the vegetable counter, the canned-goods section, *etc.*) and the operations (bringing goods to the counter, the clerk adding the price of each item, ringing up the sale, *etc.*) of the store—particularly the supermarket. Later, the children, under the teacher's guidance, may make simple purchases.

The writer, in his work with the children, has found that bringing the store to the classroom, i.e., "playing store," is a worthwhile activity for several reasons. It affords the children an opportunity to handle coins in a simulated "real-life" situation, and it acquaints them with store procedure. It provides the teacher with opportunities for impressing the students with the importance of accuracy in making purchases and handling coins. Finally, it is an excellent source of motivation.

As far as materials are concerned, playing store should offer no difficulties. A toy cash register can be used; in appearance and operation, it should approximate a real one. Numerous materials in the classroom may be used as goods. A package of writing paper may be used as a box of cookies, and a glass jar may be used as a bottle of milk. (Toy groceries may be purchased from school suppliers.) The children can bring in used grocery items from home, e.g., empty egg cartoons, milk containers, empty cans with labels, and empty cereal boxes. When the store is set up, a child is given a certain amount of pennies (no more than ten in the beginning; at a later date, larger amounts and other denominations may be used). The teacher asks the student to purchase several food items. For example, the student may be asked to buy a loaf of bread and a bottle of milk. In the beginning, the students should not purchase more than two items. The child who has been selected for the errand comes to the store and greets the storekeeper (played, at first, by the teacher). Then the child states his business. When the child has finished his order, the storekeeper adds the price of each item; he does this aloud. The prices, of course, will be unrelated to actual prices. In the beginning, for example, bread may cost two cents, a dozen eggs three cents, *etc.* The child should be expected to pay the storekeeper the exact amount, *not a penny more or less.* If a child makes a mistake in either paying or making a purchase, e.g., if a child forgets to ask for an item he was sent for, or states an item incorrectly—"a bottle of bread"—he loses his turn and someone else is sent to the store. Help the students develop the attitude that shopping must be correct from beginning to end.

C.S.R.C.
C.S.R.C.

section 2

Motor Skills

A number of studies have shown that educable mentally retarded children are below normal in motor aptitudes. In a series of motor tests given to 284 mentally retarded youngsters, Francis and Rarick* demonstrated that in comparison to mentally normal children, the retarded youngsters were markedly deficient in strength, balance, and agility. The same study concluded that a retarded child usually lags two to four years behind the mentally normal child in motor performance.

But, judging from the few experimental studies on the improvement of motor abilities of the mentally retarded as the result of training, it seems that with practice retarded youngsters can heighten motor performance and make continued improvement. Corder† and several other researchers suggest that a systematic physical training program for retarded children can result in significant gains in motor proficiency.

Although motor aptitudes of educable retarded children have been extensively investigated, little exploration has been

---

*R. J. Francis and G. L. Rarick, "Motor Characteristics of the Mentally Retarded," *American Journal of Mental Deficiency 63* (1959): 792-811.

†W. Owens Corder, "Effects of Physical Education on the Intellectual, Physical and Social Development of Educable Mentally Retarded Boys," *Exceptional Children 32* (1966): 357-364.

CHART 7. Physical Fitness Performances of Six Severely Retarded Boys

Name	Age	Pullups		Situps		Standing Broad Jump		Fifty-Yard Dash	
		Accomplished	Passing	Accomplished	Passing	Accomplished	Passing	Accomplished	Passing
Jim M.	8	0	—	6	—	2′6″	—	14.9 sec.	—
Thomas F. (dowsyn)	10	0	2	8	30	2′2″	4′8″	12.8 sec.	8.6 sec.
Ronnie M.	10	0	2	5	30	3′9″	4′8″	10.0 sec.	8.6 sec.
Alan P. (dowsyn)	12	0	2	6	37	1′10″	5′4″	13.5 sec.	8.0 sec.
Alan G. (dowsyn)	14	0	4	10	44	1′10″	6′1″	9.9 sec.	7.3 sec.
Ed K. (dowsyn)	16	1	6	13	50	5′6″	6′11″	8.9 sec.	6.8 sec.

done in this area with severely retarded youngsters. However, it is obvious that this group of children are deficient in motor development. In order to learn more accurately the extent of the children's motor deficiency, the teacher obtained validated standards of physical performance for mentally normal children from the American Association for Health, Physical Education and Recreation in Washington, D.C. These validated standards were for physical fitness tests which included pullups, situps, standing broad jump, and the fifty-yard dash. The tests covered a 10-17 age range.

Four of these tests were given to the boys in the class, and chart 7 indicates the results.

Another test was given to determine the children's senses of balance. A board measuring 6 feet in length and 10 inches in width was set on top of two 4-inch wooden blocks. The boys were asked to walk along the length of the board balancing themselves. The following chart indicates the results:

CHART 8. Balance Performance of Six Severely Retarded Boys

	Age	Walking across	Side-stepping across	Assisted
Jim M.	8			√
Thomas F.	10			√
Ronnie M.	10			√
Alan P.	12		√	
Alan G.	14		√	
Ed K.	16		√	

The tests showed that the children were far below normal in physical strength, coordination, and balance. They were severely physically handicapped, as well as severely mentally handicapped. Obviously, a program of motor development that went beyond the usual recreation period was needed; the children's physical underdevelopment called for a good deal more than organized or "free" play.

The following two units for motor development, Scouting and Shop, are clearly experimental, certainly not definitive. Being tentatively developed, the various aspects of the units may be refined and further developed, and the individual teacher is encouraged to do so. These two units are not designed to supplant present programs for motor development; rather, they are intended to supplement such programs. Thus, the units do not represent an attempt to meet all the physical needs of the children. Essentially, the Scouting chapter may be used for gross motor development, and the Shop chapter for finer motor development.

chapter 5

Scouting

This unit includes activities to develop strength, endurance, coordination, balance, and agility. Specific physical skills may be developed: jumping, climbing stairs, and tieing knots; better posture is one of the goals of the unit. Social and self-help skills may be interwoven throughout the unit. In addition, handicrafts and nature study may also be included as related activities.

This unit is designed for both boys and girls. If possible, there should be two separate patrols, one for boys, the other for girls. A patrol is a small working group within a troop (the whole class). A class troop would include both a Boy Scout and a Girl Scout patrol, each with an assigned patrol leader and assistant.* A patrol should have at least three members; if there are less than three girls (or boys) in the class, they necessarily will have to be included in the one patrol.

It is suggested that new patrol leaders and assistants be chosen every few weeks, thus giving all students a chance at these positions, as well as further motivating the youngsters. Patrol leaders and assistants should be encouraged to set an example of good behavior and effort and to guide and assist less capable students in their patrol. Specific responsibilities of patrol leaders and assistants will be suggested to the teacher as the class becomes involved in the activities outlined in this chapter.

*This organization parallels the basic organization of Boy and Girl Scouts.

STAGE 1—INTRODUCTION TO SCOUTING

PURPOSE

1. To acquaint the children with the activities and principles of Scouting
2. To motivate the children towards participating in the initial activities of the unit

MATERIALS

1. For the students: pictures and photographs of Scouting activities
2. For the teacher: a copy of the *Wolf Cub Scout Book* and the *Junior Girl Scout Handbook;* also, refer to *Scouting for the Mentally Retarded.*

METHOD

Since the children will have only a sketchy idea of Scouting, visual aids, such as pictures from magazines, photographs, and films, would be useful; if possible, field trips are an additional means by which students can become acquainted with the activities of Scouting. A class trip to a Boy Scout or Girl Scout troop meeting or a visit by several uniformed Boy or Girl Scouts to show equipment and to explain some of their activities would be helpful.

To reinforce these experiences and to further motivate the children, related art activities can be introduced. For example, drawings can be made showing different camping activities at a Scout camp.

STAGE 2—INITIAL PARTICIPATION IN SCOUTING

PURPOSE

1. To teach the children the Scout promise
2. To teach the Scout sign

METHOD

The Scout promise is: "I promise to do my best."* The children should understand what the Scout promise means. Tell the class, "When you

*This is a shortened version of the Cub Scout and Brownie Promises. The Cub Scout Promise: "I, (name), promise to do my best to do my duty to God and my country, to be square and obey the Law of the Pack." (The Cub Scout motto is "Do your best.") The Brownie Promise: "I promise to do my best to love God and my country, to help other people every day, especially those at home." For a class of older severely retarded youngsters, the teacher may wish to use this modified version of the Girl Scout and Boy Scout oath: "I promise to help other people at all times, and I promise to keep myself strong, ready and good."

promise to do something, you mean you will do it. I will do my best means I will try as hard as I can." Point out that a Scout keeps his or her promise.

Have the class stand and give the Scout promise at the beginning of each Scouting lesson. Each time the Scout promise is said, both boys and girls should give the Scout sign:

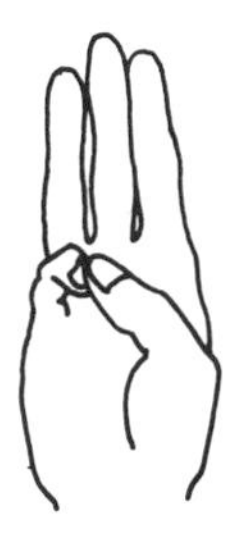

FIGURE 5-1.

Some of the youngsters, particularly dowsyn children, may find it difficult to keep the three middle fingers extended while joining the thumb and little finger. In this case, the sign can be made with two fingers, the index and middle fingers, raised. Whether the sign is made with two or three fingers,* the whole class should give the same Scout sign.

If the Pledge of Allegiance is said each morning, the children may give the Scout salute. For boys, the Scout salute is similar to the regular military salute except that three fingers are extended and the thumb and little finger are joined as in the Scout sign (or, if the boys are making the Scout sign with two fingers extended, then two fingers are extended in the salute). For girls, the Scout salute is similar to the citizen's salute — the hand placed over the heart with three fingers (or two) extended.

The teacher should find the Scout quiet sign useful for the Scouting activities and for other activities. Without speaking, the teacher simply raises her hand high, and as soon as a child sees her hand, he stops whatever he (or she) is doing or saying and raises his (or her) hand. Soon, all the children in the class will have their hands raised; the room should be quiet. Some Scout leaders form the Scout sign when they raise their hand, and the children respond by raising their hands and giving the same sign. Whether the hand is simply raised or the hand is raised in the Scout sign,

*In both Boy Scouts and Girl Scouts, the younger Scouts make the sign with two fingers extended; older Scouts use three fingers. An even simpler Scout sign, suggested in *Scouting for the Mentally Retarded,* is to have the child join his thumb with his index finger as in the familiar "OK" sign.

the teacher should find the Scout quiet sign effective in the classroom and on the playground.*

STAGE 3—TIEING A SIMPLE KNOT

PURPOSE

1. To teach both boys and girls how to tie an overhand knot
2. To teach the children the fundamental operation involved in tieing their shoelaces
3. To develop finger dexterity and coordination

MATERIALS

Strands of rope or twine about 16 inches in length.

METHOD

Discuss the importance of knot tieing in Scouting. Perhaps a Boy or Girl Scout can visit the class to demonstrate the tieing of different knots.

Pass out the twine. Stand with your back at about a 45 degree angle to the class, demonstrating the tieing of an overhand knot above your left shoulder. Proceed, step by step, with the children performing each step with you.

STEP-BY-STEP PROCEDURE IN TIEING AN OVERHAND KNOT

The strand of twine is held several inches from each end, palms upward.

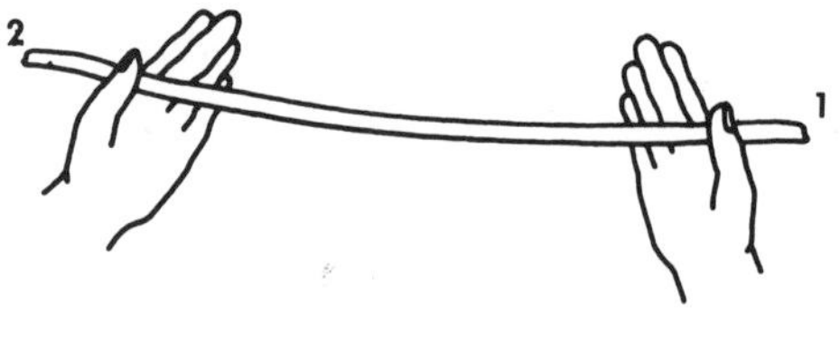

2

1

FIGURE 5-2.

*Strive for instant silence and attention. To this end, as suggested in *Scouting for the Mentally Retarded,* a game can be made of this activity. "It took you too long this time. We'll try it again. Now, back to work." Then a few seconds later give the Scout quiet sign again. "That was better. But let's try to do it even faster."

The ends are crossed, with end number 2 on the inside, closest to the body, forming a loop which is held in place at the point where the ends cross by the thumb and forefinger of the left hand.

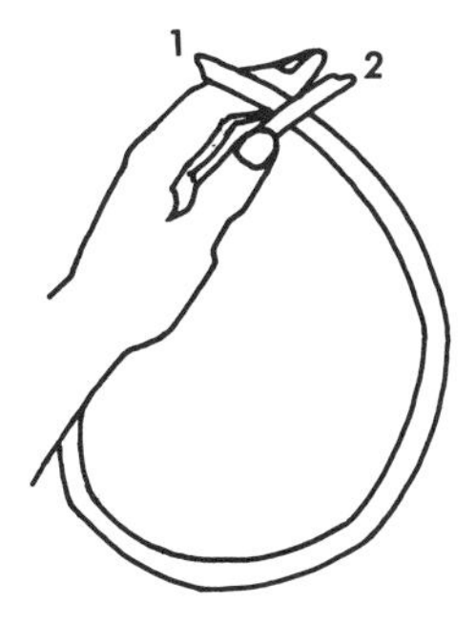

FIGURE 5-3.

The right hand is placed inside the loop.

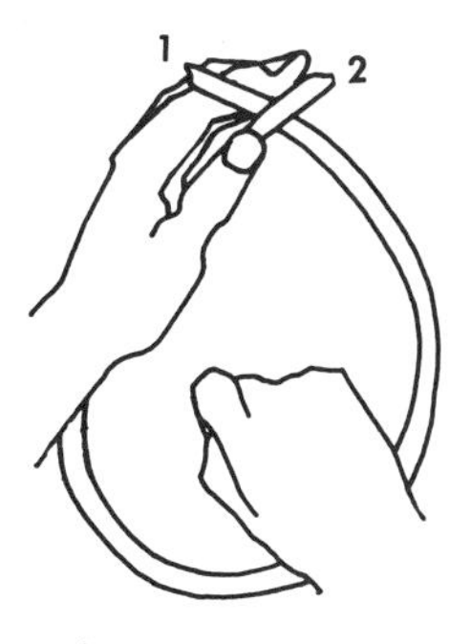

FIGURE 5-4.

The thumb and forefinger of the right hand grasp end number 2, and this end is pulled slightly toward the body.

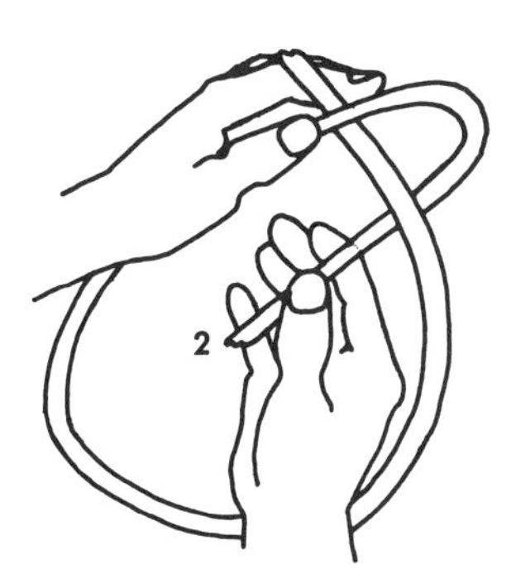

FIGURE 5-5.

The thumb and forefinger of the left hand grasp end number 1, then both ends are pulled.*

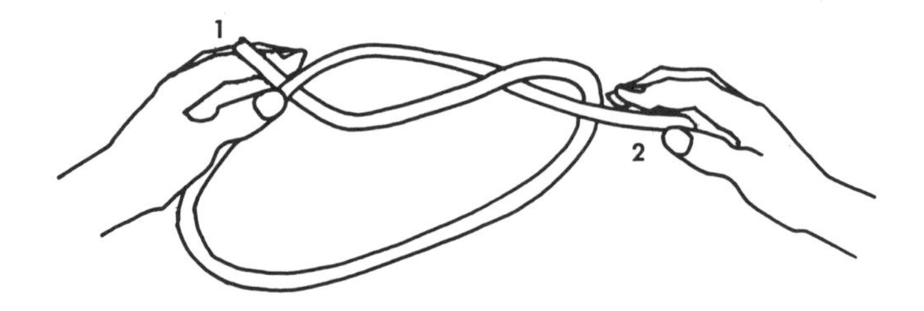

FIGURE 5-6.

RESULT

Normally intelligent children generally have little difficulty learning to tie a simple knot; for severely retarded children, it is, of course, a very difficult task. The children have poor finger coordination, and the knot configurations are confusing to them. It is essential, therefore, that the task be taught step by step. The children will need a great deal of practice in this activity; it may take weeks or months before they are able to tie a simple knot.

STAGE 4—POSTURE

PURPOSE

1. To provide the children with standards of good posture in sitting, standing and walking
2. To make the children aware of any poor posture habits they may have
3. To motivate the children towards improving their own posture

*In *Scouting for the Mentally Retarded,* it is suggested that, as an instructional aid, opposite ends of the rope be taped with different colors. Instructions would be given accordingly, "Take hold of the red end, *etc.*"

METHOD

It will be noted that the above purposes do not include having the teacher correct poor posture. Poor posture is often the result of habit, and habit is not easily changed. Certainly, the teacher will point out posture faults and attempt to help students correct these problems, but it would be unrealistic to assume that such a procedure would affect anything more than a momentary improvement.

In a realistic program of posture improvement, the teacher must emphasize good posture as a standard, then have the children evaluate their own posture in light of this standard, and finally motivate them to change poor posture habits.

Good posture is not characterized by military-type stiffness, but by correct body alignment. When a person stands correctly his body parts are in vertical alignment. Thus, an imaginary line would come down the center of his head, neck, hips and knees to his ankles:

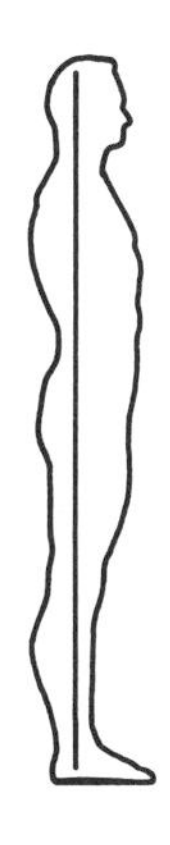

FIGURE 5-7.

When a person sits correctly, the alignment of his body parts would represent two 90 degree angles.

Life-sized enlargements can be made of the standing and sitting silhouettes as illustrated in figures 5-7 and 5-8. The enlargements should be hung in the classroom. Also, a student, or the teacher herself, can regularly demonstrate the correct standing and sitting posture.

Making the boys and girls aware of their individual posture deficiencies is quite difficult. Full-length mirrors would be helpful, but it is unlikely

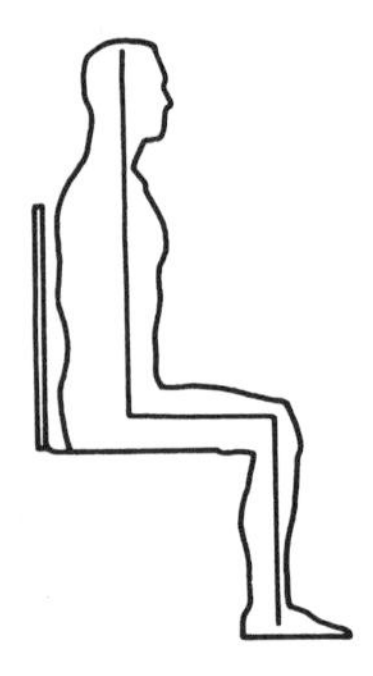

FIGURE 5-8.

that they would be available. The most practical course would be to point out, as tactfully as possible, poor posture elements in individual students. By this time, there should be enough rapport between the children and teacher for them not to feel uncomfortable or embarrassed by her speaking to them about their individual posture problems. Thus, a positive response from the children can be expected.

Some of the children may have nonremedial postural irregularities. Flat feet are not uncommon among children. Dowsyn children characteristically have sloping hollow backs and prominent abdomens. *The teacher should concentrate on those postural elements that can be improved.* Some children in the class may be suffering from obesity; this, of course, has an adverse affect on posture. In such cases, therefore, the teacher might suggest that the parents consult a doctor for a suitable and safe diet.

POOR POSTURE ELEMENTS

A. Sitting
   1. Upper back and hips not touching the back of the chair
   2. Chest lowered
   3. Lower legs not vertical
   4. Feet not flat on the floor

B. Standing
   1. Head forward
   2. Shoulders rounded

3. Chest lowered
4. Abdomen prominent
5. Sloping hollow back
6. Knees not straight
7. Body weight not slightly forward (over the balls of the feet)

C. Walking
1. Head forward
2. Eyes not level, head to side
3. Shoulders rounded
4. Chest lowered
5. Arms not swinging freely
6. Abdomen prominent
7. Sloping hollow back
8. Shuffling, not lifting feet from ground
9. Toes pointed outward instead of straight ahead

Throughout the unit, the teacher should impress the children with the thought that having good posture is part of being a Scout. "That is not the way a Boy Scout sits, Greg." "A Boy Scout sits straight, like this." "That is not the way a Girl Scout stands, Carol," etc.

The unit itself will indirectly affect an improvement in the children's posture. Some elements of poor posture are due to lack of strength and coordination, and building up strength and coordination are major purposes of the unit. Simple exercises and games can be conducted that are specifically developed to improve posture. The following exercises and games are suggested.

Stop and Go. The children pretend they are stop and go signals in the middle of the street. They stand with arms straight out from their sides. To signal "Go," they face the front; to signal "Stop," they face the side. The teacher directs movements by calling for "Stop" and "Go." Encourage them to alternate swinging left and right for the "Stop" signal. Stress trunk twisting and arm extension at shoulder height.

Row the Boat. Starting position: the children stand with elbows raised to shoulder height and fists clinched, almost touching, and palms down in front of their chest. They thrust elbows back *hard*, then return to starting position. Throughout this exercise, be sure the children keep heads erect and elbows up at shoulder height. In the beginning, this exercise should be done with the children.

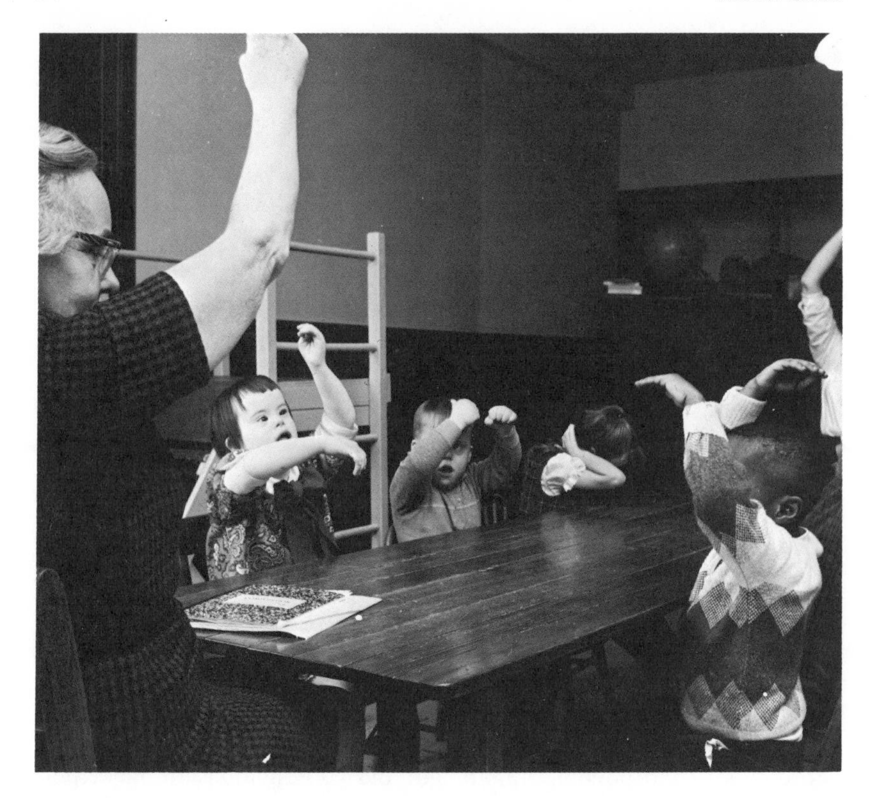

Up to the Sky. Starting position: children are at attention — standing erect, arms down at their sides. They swing arms forward and upward to a full stretch over head and, at the same time, rise high on their toes. Then they swing their arms to the side and down slowly, at the same time coming down on their heels. The teacher should not expect all the students to do this exercise correctly the first time. Some children, in the beginning, may have difficulty coordinating their movements.

Circles. Starting position: children stand, arms extended sideways at shoulder height, palms up. They slowly circle the hands upward and backward, making circles about a foot in diameter, pressing the arms backward. Then palms are turned down and circles are made forward.

Funny Hat Race. This is a relay race and should be played outside or in the gym. Two teams line up at a starting line. The first player of each team places an eraser or book on his head and, on the signal "Go," walks or runs to a predetermined line and back. Hands may not be used to reset the eraser. If it falls off the head, the child must go back to the starting line. When the child returns with the eraser on his head, he gives it to the second player who repeats the action. (The first player goes to the end of the line.) The first team to complete the relay is the winner. As preparation for this activity, the children can practice walking the width of the classroom with an eraser or book on their heads.

Pull-Up. Starting position: children place arms overhead, fists clinched. They pull their arms down slowly, as though they were chinning, until their fists are by their shoulders. Repeat.

Flying. Starting position: standing, children lean forward from the waist, arms hanging loosely from their shoulders. Still leaning forward, they swing their arms sideways and back hard, holding this position for a second or two, then they return to the starting position.

Wings Back. Starting position: children stand with fingertips touching their shoulders, elbows in front of body. They move their arms out and back until their elbows hug their sides. They hold this position a second or two while trying to force their arms further back, then they return to the starting position.

Hands Up. This exercise should be done in the gym or on the playfield. Starting position: children sit on the floor with feet down, knees raised; they bend forward from the waist and stretch their arms forward. Still leaning forward, they swing their arms upward and backward; then they return to the starting position.

Wheelbarrow Race. This activity should be done in the gym or on the playfield. Children pair off; preferably partners should be about equal in height. A child puts his hands on the starting line, his feet apart. His partner lifts his legs by grasping his knees. In this position, they move forward. Caution the standing partner to keep his arms down at his sides and not to move faster than the "wheelbarrow" partner. The latter should keep his weight on his hands and his arms stiff. The first pair to reach the finish line wins the race.

STAGE 5—INTRODUCTION TO THE HIKE

PURPOSE

1. To develop physical balance
2. To motivate the children towards participation in the classroom "hike"

MATERIALS

Six or more two-by-four boards approximately 8 inches long. ("Two-by-four" is the name given to standard-sized lumber commonly used in wood construction; it actually measures 1½ inches by 3½ inches.)

METHOD

The teacher sets the two-by-fours on the classroom floor in an area of the room that is free of furniture. The boards or blocks are set in this manner:

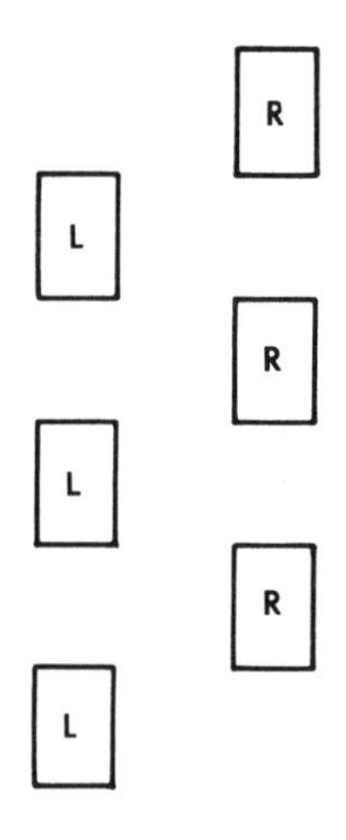

FIGURE 5-9.

At first, the boards may be set about 20 inches from each other.

The teacher reminds the students that Boy Scouts and Girl Scouts go on hikes and that sometimes they have to cross a stream by stepping on stones. "Today we are going to pretend that we are going on a hike and must cross a stream. We will pretend that these blocks are stones set across the stream. This is how you will cross." Demonstrate. Then have individual students attempt it. Of course, the teacher will stand by to assist when necessary. However, the children should be encouraged to "cross the stream" unassisted, since the purpose of the activity is to give them practice in balance.

When the children have developed some ability in this activity, the pieces may be spaced at gradually increasing distances; for example:

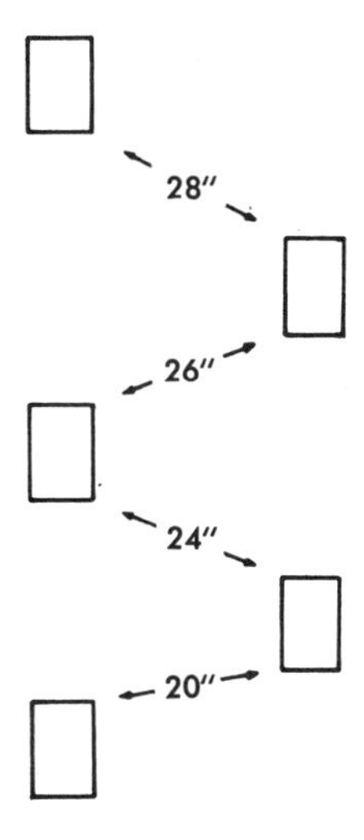

FIGURE 5-10.

RESULT

The children will enjoy this activity. Dowsyn children in particular seem to enjoy pretending. It is suggested that the teacher record the children's original performances, then at subsequent times, she may retest the children to determine exactly what progress they have made.

STAGE 6—THE CLASSROOM HIKE

PURPOSE

1. To develop coordination, balance, and agility
2. To develop the ability to jump and to climb steps properly

MATERIALS

Classroom furniture and equipment

METHOD

The teacher will use whatever classroom furniture and equipment are available. In every classroom there are items which can be used for the purposes of this unit. Of course, the teacher's ingenuity will be challenged in finding and utilizing classroom items.

The following are some suggested items:

Item 1 — flannel board. A flannel board may represent low tree branches. It is simply stood in an open position, and students pass underneath.

FIGURE 5-11.

Item 2 — practice steps. This item is standard equipment in many class rooms for younger retarded children. It may represent a hill. With the teacher standing by, the students climb the hill, then jump down.

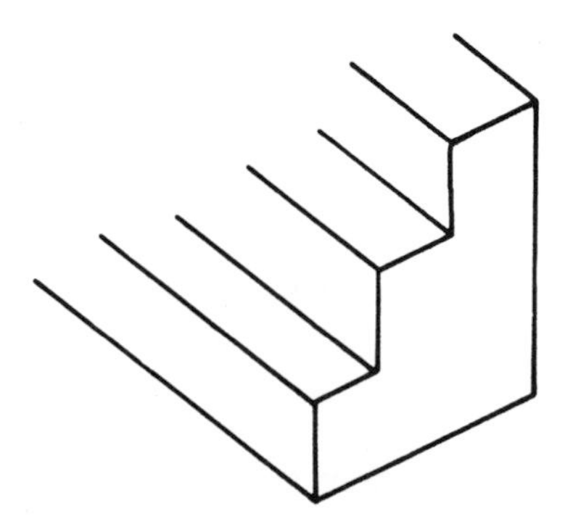

FIGURE 5-12.

Item 3 — pyramid steps. This item is actually the base of a see-saw. It may represent a pile of rocks. The children walk up each rung, balancing themselves.

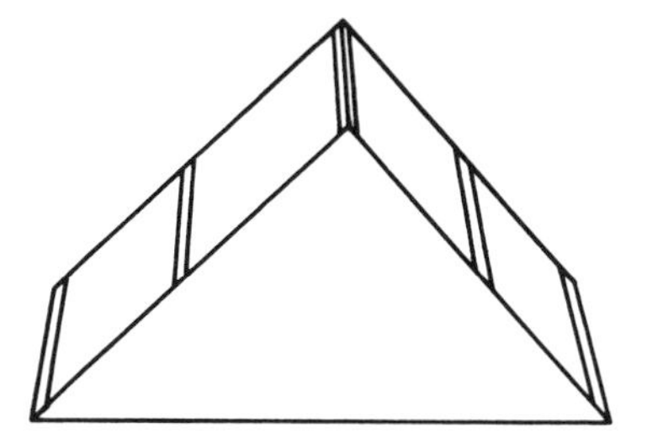

FIGURE 5-13.

Item 4 — table. This is simply a regular classroom table. It may represent a cliff. The students go along the top on their hands and knees, then step down.

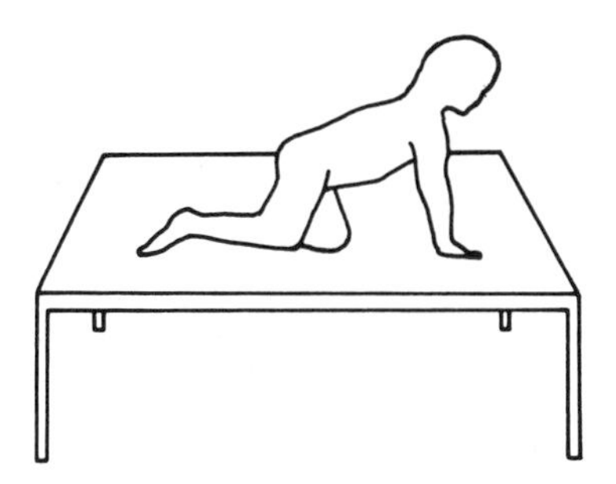

FIGURE 5-14.

Item 5 — board. Any strong board can be used.* It should measure approximately 6 feet in length and 8 to 10 inches in width. It may represent a log across a stream. It can be set across two wooden blocks about 4 inches in height or across two *low* chairs. As a precaution, the teacher should stand alongside the board.

*Walking boards and balance beams can be purchased. Walking boards are usually 9 inches wide; balance beams are approximately 1 to 4 inches wide and may be used with older, more physically advanced children. The top of a see-saw can be used too.

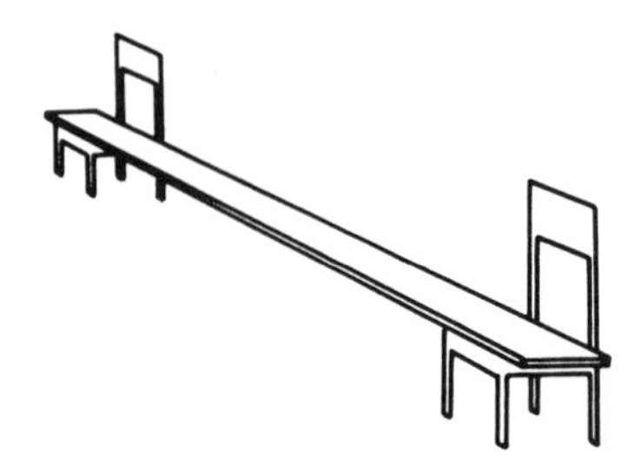

FIGURE 5-15.

Item 6 — classroom (kindergarten) cot. This is a standard item in many classrooms for younger severely retarded children. It may be used to represent very low tree branches. The students move under the cot and crawl its length (of course, a mat of some kind should be placed underneath).

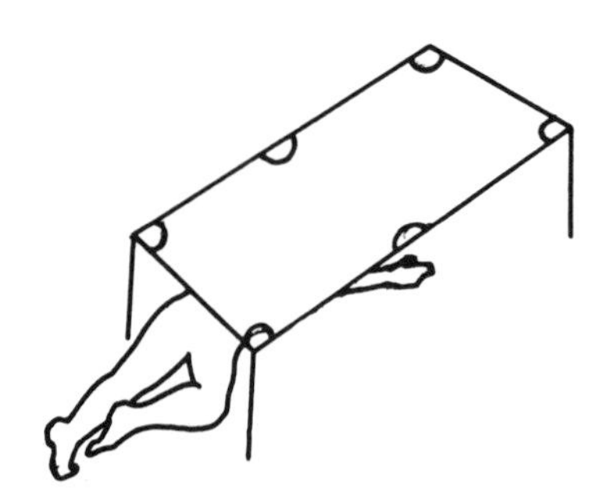

FIGURE 5-16.

Item 7 — yardstick. This is placed across any two objects in the classroom to represent a low tree branch.

Item 8 — a wastebasket. Turned upside down, a wastebasket may represent a tree stump. Have the children step up on it, then step down on the other side.

Item 9 — classroom play equipment — stove, cupboard, refrigerator, etc. These items may be arranged as a maze.

In addition, the teacher can draw two nearly parallel lines on the floor with chalk. The children can jump across the "stream." If the stream is

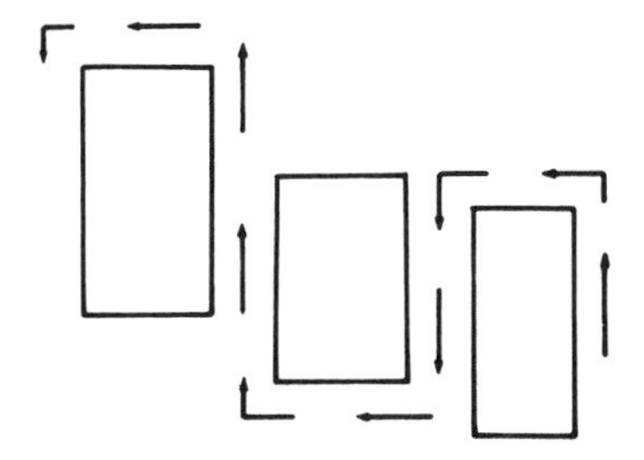

FIGURE 5-17.

narrow, the children should jump across from a standing broad jump. Only two or three of these items should be introduced in the beginning; later, other items may be added to the hike.

The children should clearly understand how they are to proceed through each obstacle in the hike. In climbing the hill, they should be encouraged to go up by alternating feet, instead of placing both feet on each step. In jumping down from the hill, both feet should leave the top at the same time, rather than one foot moving off before the other. For reasons of safety, both feet should reach the ground at the same time, and, upon reaching the ground, the knees should be flexed to absorb the weight of the body.

In going along the log over the stream, the children should be encouraged to walk across, instead of inching their way by side-stepping.

Of course, the teacher should stand by the potentially dangerous obstacles. Lest the classroom hike seem dangerous for severly retarded children, it should be pointed out that in the many hikes taken by the children in the writer's class, no child was ever injured. It is recommended, for both safety and comfort, that the children wear sneakers for the hiking activities and that the girls wear slacks or shorts.

In setting up the obstacles for the hike, three sides of the classroom may be used in the manner shown in figure 5-18.*

The advantages of such an arrangement are:

1. It provides free movement for the children from obstacle to obstacle

*The teacher may use any obstacles she wishes and in any order she prefers.

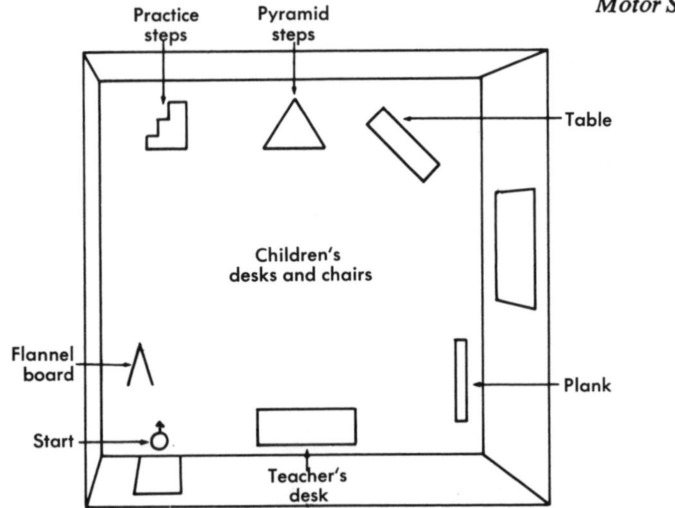

FIGURE 5-18. Suggested Arrangement for Classroom "Hike"

2. It permits the teacher to observe easily the children as they go through the hike
3. The space required is relatively small, but is sufficient for a varied and interesting series of obstacles
4. It does not disturb the arrangement of desks and chairs
5. The equipment can easily be set up and put away

In going on the hike, the children should proceed in single file as a patrol, led by the patrol leader.

RESULT

The children will enjoy this activity; and the teacher should find it a valuable means of determining specific physical deficiencies. Of course, the hike can also be used to help meet such deficiencies, and, in time, the teacher may want to introduce varied developmental activities centered around the hike.

STAGE 7—DEVELOPMENTAL ACTIVITIES (1)

PURPOSE

To develop balance and coordination

MATERIALS

1. Items for obstacles in the hike*
2. A scarf or large handkerchief
3. Four two-by-four blocks, each approximately 8 inches in length (several dictionaries may be substituted)

METHOD

The two-by-four blocks (or the dictionaries) are placed inside the scarf. Grasping the corners of the scarf, a child slings it over his shoulders like a sack; carrying the sack in this manner, the child proceeds through the hike. Because this extra burden requires the children to move carefully and slowly through the hike, it places a greater demand on muscles to balance and coordinate their bodies.

RESULT

At first the children will find it difficult to proceed with the extra burden, but with practice they should move with comparative ease, reflecting an improvement in body balance and coordination.

DEVELOPMENTAL ACTIVITIES (2)

PURPOSE

To develop agility

MATERIALS

The same as developmental activities (1)

---

*By the time the teacher introduces developmental activities, there probably will be four or five items which will be regularly used as obstacles for the hike.

METHOD

A boy or girl is selected to be the injured Scout. The child goes through the hike and immediately after the last obstacle pretends to have twisted an ankle. The child calls for help. Another Scout, carrying the weighted sack of first aid supplies (actually includes a strip of gauze), goes to the rescue, moving through the hike swiftly. Reaching the first Scout, the second Scout sets the first aid supplies down, takes out the strip of gauze and ties it around the injured Scout's ankle; then he helps the child up.

RESULT

This is a useful developmental activity since the children try to get to the injured Scout as quickly as they can. Thus, it is a means of developing agility, as well as balance and coordination.

To note the progress in these areas, the teacher can keep a daily record of the time it takes the children to complete "the mission."

The children should enjoy this activity and should participate with enthusiasm. Some children will even play the part of the injured Scout as though they were performing a deathbed scene in a soap opera.

DEVELOPMENTAL ACTIVITIES (3)

PURPOSE

To develop agility

MATERIALS

The regular items of the hike

METHOD

Game — "Indian and Bear." A child is selected to be the bear, another child is the Indian. The Indian stands in front of the bear at the starting point of the hike. As soon as the teacher says, “Go!” the Indian gives a yell (Indian-style) and begins to move swiftly through the hike. A few seconds later the teacher again says, “Go!” and the bear gives a fierce growl and sets off through the hike in pursuit of the Indian.

DEVELOPMENTAL ACTIVITIES (4)

PURPOSE

To develop strength and endurance

MATERIALS

The regular items of the hike

METHOD

A Scout pretends to be ill. He or she must be taken to the first-aid station. In order to get there, the Scout must be carried through the hike on a stretcher (the classroom cot) and the stretcher is carried by four Boy Scouts.

RESULT

This is a difficult activity, but it should challenge the children’s strength and endurance, and it should provide them with a good deal of fun.

The first attempt at this activity provided a memorable experience for the class. With the first obstacle, the flannel board (low branches), the four boys carrying the stretcher faced a problem — how to get the stretcher under the flannel board. For a moment, the boys stood helpless, then the teacher suggested they tilt the stretcher a bit. Taking a firm grip on the cot, the boys turned the stretcher sideways and the startled patient tumbled off, to the great amusement of the class, including the quickly-recovered patient.

DEVELOPMENTAL ACTIVITIES (5)

PURPOSE

To develop muscular control

MATERIALS

The regular items of the hike

METHOD

Game—"Night Patrol." The classroom blinds are closed, and the lights are turned off. The children line up in patrol formation then, moving as quietly as they can, they proceed through the hike.

Game — "Scout and Indian." The classroom is darkened. A child is selected as the Scout dozing before the campfire; select another child as the Indian. The Scout sits in the center of the classroom, a cap pulled down over his eyes. The Indian must try to go through the hike as quietly as possible, come up behind the Scout, yell, and lift the Scout's cap. If the Scout hears the Indian coming towards him, he raises the cap from his eyes, points, and yells, "Indian!"

RESULT

The children in the writer's class found these activities exciting, particularly "Scout and Indian." The children, at first, found it very difficult to move quietly through the obstacles; but gradually, they became aware of the noise they were making (in a darkened, quiet room, a creaking stair, for example, can easily break the silence). In time, they became increasingly skilled at controlling their movements.

CONCLUSION

By the time he begins school, the normally intelligent child has had extensive physical experiences in jumping, climbing, balancing, and other basic motor activities. The severely retarded child of beginning school age, on the other hand, has had severely limited physical experiences. Furthermore, due to his lack of companionship, it is unlikely that during his school years he will have opportunities for many physically active experiences outside of school. The unit on Scouting, therefore, will provide the severely retarded child with such physical experiences as jumping, climbing, and balancing, which he otherwise would have little opportunity to enjoy, and these experiences will help develop and improve motor skills.

A great advantage of a unit on Scouting is that it inspires self-motivation in the children. Although they may have only a vague idea of what Scouting is about, they are apt to identify this activity with normally intelligent children. It is natural, therefore, that the children should be interested and want to succeed in the unit. Also, it affords them a sense of self-esteem, which they so often deeply lack.

What can the children achieve in the unit? Based on the teacher's observations and records, these were the results of some of the children's work in the unit:

James M., an eight-year-old brain-injured boy. In the beginning, James moved awkwardly under the flannel board, took the steps with both feet on each step, was afraid to jump down and had to be assisted in jumping, was unable to balance himself on the pyramid steps, and had to be assisted across the "log." Within several months, James could move easily under the flannel board, could climb the steps with alternating feet, jump confidently and unassisted, balance himself on the pyramid steps, and walk across the "log" unassisted.

Ronald M., a ten-year-old brain-injured boy. At first, Ronald could move easily through the obstacles, except for those requiring balance; on both the pyramid steps and the "log," he had to be assisted. Within a few months, he could go through these two obstacles easily and unassisted.

Thomas F., a ten-year-old dowsyn boy. In the beginning, Thomas could not climb the steps properly; he had to be assisted in jumping from the steps, in going over the pyramid steps, and in going across the "log." In several months, Thomas could climb the steps with alternating feet, jump down unassisted, balance himself on the pyramid steps, and sidestep the plank unassisted.

Alan P., a twelve-year-old dowsyn boy. At first, Alan could not climb the steps properly, was afraid and had to be assisted in jumping, was unable to balance himself on the pyramid steps, and could move across the "log" only by sidestepping. In a few months, Alan could climb the steps with alternating feet, jump unassisted, balance himself on the pyramid steps, and walk, one foot after the other, the length of the "log."

Alan G., a fourteen-year-old dowsyn boy. In the beginning, Alan moved awkwardly under the flannel board, climbed the steps by putting both feet on the same step, was afraid and had to be assisted in jumping down, was unable to balance himself on the pyramid steps, and had to inch his way along the "log" by sidestepping. In several months, Alan could move easily under the flannel board, properly climb the steps, jump down confidently and without assistance, balance himself on the pyramid steps, and walk the length of the "log" unassisted.

Ed. K., a sixteen-year-old dowsyn boy. In the beginning, Ed could not balance himself on the pyramid steps and could only move across the "log" by sidestepping. In a few months, Ed could balance himself on the pyramid steps and walk across the plank easily and confidently.

The children's progress in coordination, balance, climbing, and jumping is suggested by their agility performances in going through the obstacles of the hike. The following chart indicates the time it took six children to go through the five regular obstacles of the hike:

CHART 9. Agility Performance of Six Severely Retarded Boys (December 17, 1961 to April 3, 1962)

	Dec. 17	Jan. 24	Feb. 6	Feb. 23	March 20	April 3
Jim M. 8 yrs. old	1:30	1:45	51	1:00	23	27
Thomas F. 10 yrs. old	1:00	27	43	(absent)	32	32
Ronnie M. 10 yrs. old	25	12	19	12	18	15
Alan P. 12 yrs. old	17	40	23	20	20	19
Alan G. 14 yrs. old	(absent)	46	38	17	29	31
Ed K. 16 yrs. old	35	40	26	15	17	14

It will be noted that between the first and last dates the boys were tested, three boys substantially reduced the time it took them to get through the hike: Jim M. reduced his time to about one-third of what it was originally; Thomas F. and Ed K. reduced their times to approximately half of their original times. (It took a non-retarded nine-year-old boy, totally unfamiliar with the hike, nine seconds to go through it.)

The classroom hike is the central activity of the unit. The teacher will spend much of her time in the unit perfecting, developing, and structuring it. Each obstacle of the hike should serve a specific purpose. For example, the board set across two chairs is to develop balance; the "maze" is to develop agility; and crawling under the cot is to develop coordination. In selecting items of her own, the teacher should ask herself what physical purpose the obstacle would serve. The teacher, of course, should be guided by the children's needs in selecting obstacles. The children are apt to need development in a number of physical skills; theoretically, therefore, the teacher could start almost anywhere. However, the program should be focused on the greatest physical deficiencies of most of the children.

The teacher should keep a record of the children's performance on the obstacles. This record could include specific performance characteristics; e.g., that a child exhibits fear in climbing the steps or that a child climbs the steps by putting both feet on the same step. From time to time throughout the unit, the children's accomplishments should be recorded. In doing this the teacher will know, in fact, whether progress has been made by individual students.

The Scouting unit is primarily for developing gross motor skills, but it also offers opportunities for the development of social adjustment and self-help skills. *Throughout the unit,* the teacher should stress the Scouting standards — a Scout is helpful, friendly, courteous, kind, obediant, cheerful, brave, and clean. By stressing these standards, the teacher will help

develop in the children better emotional and social attitudes and encourage self-care. For example, each day, at the beginning of the Scouting activities, the teacher can call the class into patrol formation at attention, then inspect the children for cleanliness and neatness. ("A Boy Scout is clean, John; you forgot to clean your fingernails this morning." "A Girl Scout is neat, Lois; you can make your hair look nicer.") During other classroom activities the children can also be reminded of Scouting standards. ("A Boy Scout is courteous, Charles, you forgot to say 'thank you'." "A Girl Scout is helpful, Janice; would you like to help Peggy?").

Although the hike is the central activity in the unit, there are related activities which are important. The following are suggested related activities:

1. The children can make a patrol flag. They might first draw it on paper. The flag will have a symbol denoting the name of the patrol: Beaver, Eagle, Indian, Lion, Pine Tree, Wolf, Arrow, Bear, etc.*

2. Have the children collect colorful fall leaves, green leaves (from trees, bushes or ferns) or even vegetable leaves (celery, for example)† and arrange them between sheets of waxed paper. The sheets are then pressed together with an iron to make place mats, which can be used to decorate the classroom or taken home. A single leaf can be placed between two smaller sheets of waxed paper, pressed with an iron and placed on a wall in the classroom or at home for decoration. Treated this way, the leaves will last for years.

3. Have the children draw a map of their school, indicating the location of the main entrance, the principal's office, their classroom, the cafeteria, the gym, the library, etc.

4. Using copper or silver wire, the children can make wire bracelets and necklaces. The wire can be shaped and twisted by hand into different designs. The designs, of course, should be simple. A small open loop at one end can serve as a catch. A form can be made for bending the wire into patterns (loops and circles) by driving nails part of the way into a block of wood.

---

*Most Scout patrols are named after animals.

†The children can learn the names of the trees, bushes or vegetables from which the leaves come.

5. The teacher might have the children try the Morse Code. The dots and dashes can be made with a pencil striking the edge of their desk — a dot made by a short rap of the pencil, a dash by the pencil moving along the edge of the desk. A dictionary or encyclopedia can be referred to for the Morse Code signals.

6. The children should enjoy learning Indian sign language. The hand symbols are easy to do. The teacher may refer to the *Wolf Cub Scout Book.**

7. The children can go on a real hike, which could include crossing a stream by walking across a log, building a campfire, toasting marshmallows, and exploring nature.

8. A nature exhibit can be set up in the classroom (it could include twigs, pine cones, leaves, and wild flowers).

9. The children can work on a model camp-site (using a scale of about 1½ inches equals 3 feet).

10. Encourage the children to start shell or rock collections (cigar boxes and egg cartons serve as good cases for the collections).

Through participation in the unit on Scouting, severely retarded youngsters should acquire the knowledge, skills, and self-confidence to go on to actual Scouting. For a number of years there have been Boy Scout units for handicapped youngsters—blind, deaf, emotional disturbed, physically handicapped, and mentally retarded. According to figures from the Boy Scouts of America, there are presently 1,244 units of mentally retarded Boy Scouts—454 Cub Scout troops, 689 Boy Scout units, and 101 Explorer Scout troops, totaling 19,194 mentally retarded youngsters. Of course, the majority of these youngsters are educably retarded, but there are dowsyns and other severely retarded youngsters in Boy Scout units.

For the most part, the Boy Scouts of America has followed the special unit plan—units formed especially for retarded youngsters. This, according to the organization, makes possible "a slower paced program which can be geared to their learning ability." However, there are some opportunities for contacts with mentally normal boys through participation in summer camps, district and council activities, and intertroop visits. Several

---

**Wolf Cub Scout Book* (New Brunswick, New Jersey: Boy Scouts of America, 1967), pp. 84-85.

years ago, the Boy Scouts of America published a Scouting program guide for those who work with mentally retarded boys; copies of *Scouting for the Mentally Retarded* should be available from a local Boy Scout office.

Most of the mentally retarded girls in Scouting belong to special troops. These troops are often affiliated with local associations serving retarded children. Some retarded girls belong to neighborhood troops of mentally normal girls. The Girl Scouts of the U.S.A. usually does not recommend that severely retarded girls be included in troops of non-retarded girls. Figures are presently unavailable for the number of mentally retarded girls in the Girl Scouts. However, recent figures show a total enrollment of some 12,000 cerebral palsy, epileptic, emotionally disturbed, mentally retarded, and other handicapped girls in the program.

All Scouting units are sponsored by a group or institution. Units for retarded youngsters can be sponsored by a hospital, a residential facility, a school, a parent-teachers association or a group of parents. Information on getting a retarded boy or girl into Scouting or on getting a unit for retarded youngsters started can be obtained from a local Boy Scout or Girl Scout office.

After participation in the Scouting unit, two boys in the class were invited to join the local Boy Scout troop (both boys were dowsyns). But, the parents were undecided; they had doubts about their children's ability to keep up with normal youngsters. The parents' fears were understandable, however, perhaps because of their participation in the unit, the two boys felt confident and ready to join the troop.

chapter 6

Shop

This chapter includes activities for developing eye-hand coordination and hand and arm strength. Essentially, it provides activities for finer motor development. In addition, the children learn basic tool and woodwork skills: handling a hammer, driving and removing a nail, using a screwdriver to turn in a screw, lining up pieces of lumber for nailing, and making tie racks, small tables, and chairs.*

It seems that driving a nail and turning a screw are very difficult tasks for severely retarded children. In the teacher's severely retarded class, six boys were tested on their ability to hammer a 1½ inch common nail into a block of pine wood; it took a mentally normal 9-year-old boy 16 blows to drive in the nail. The following chart indicates the results of the same task with the severely retarded boys:

---

*This unit is a basic one in woodwork skills; therefore, both men and women teachers should be able to function confidentally in it.

CHART 10. Nailing Performance of Six Severely Retarded Boys

	Age	Number of blows
Jim M.	8	205
Thomas F. (dowsyn)	10	95
Ronnie M.	10	70
Alan P. (dowsyn)	12	25
Alan G. (dowsyn)	14	(unable)
Ed K. (dowsyn)	16	39

THE HAMMER

PURPOSE

1. To acquaint the children with the use and proper handling of the hammer and to develop proficiency in using it
2. To motivate the children towards participation in the unit
3. To develop eye-hand coordination and hand and arm strength

MATERIALS

1. Medium weight claw-hammer, 10 or 12 ounces*
2. Spare pieces of two-by-fours, approximately eight inches long
3. Boards approximately 20 inches long, 5 inches wide and ¾ to 1 inch thick†

*For the younger children, small metal claw-hammers with rubber grip handles measuring 8 inches in length.

†All the lumber for this unit may be obtained from lumber yards or building sites where end pieces of lumber have been discarded. There very likely will be no charge for scrap wood at lumber yards, particularly for school purposes.

4. 1, 1½, and 2 inch nails with regular-sized heads; shingle nails, and thumb tacks

STAGE 1—INTRODUCTION TO SHOP

METHOD

Begin by identifying the parts of the hammer:

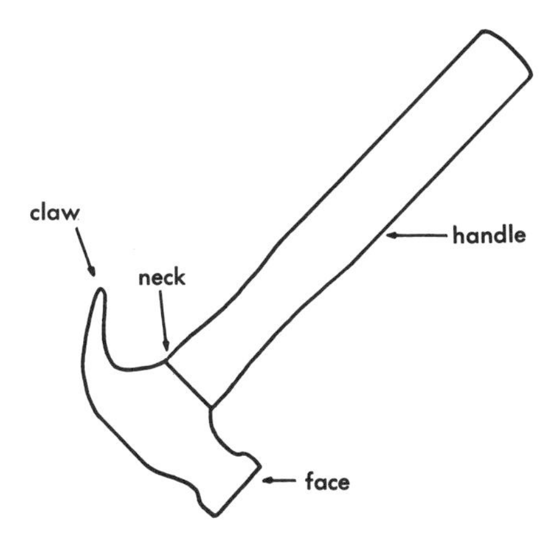

FIGURE 6-1. Hammer

Next, demonstrate how to drive a nail. The hand grips the hammer firmly at the base of the handle. When striking the nail, the handle should form a 90 degree angle with the nail to insure that the hammer face hits the nail head squarely.

Drive several nails into the two-by-four. Then call on one of the students to drive in a nail. First start the nail for the student by holding the nail with one hand and tapping it in a bit with the hammer until it is secured, then have the student drive the nail the rest of the way down.

After several students have attempted to drive in a nail, drive four or five nails ½ inch into the board. The nails should be at least 3 inches apart. Hang a tie on one of the nails, illustrating that you have made a tie rack. (A detailed explanation of how to make a tie rack is given on pp. 116-117.)

RESULT

Since this may be the first time some of the children will have handled a hammer, the results are likely to be poor. The children tend to hold the hammer high up on the handle, instead of at the base. This tendency is due to the children's lack of strength and accuracy in hitting a nail. If this tendency is very pronounced, the children may be given smaller hammers for a while.

The children should need little or no motivation. It is likely that they will be eager to participate in this unit. Therefore, the making of a tie rack at this time may not be necessary. If the tie rack is made at this time (for the purpose of motivation), the children may want to make tie racks, too. In that case, you might want to point out to the children that before they can make a tie rack and do other woodwork, they must first learn how to handle a hammer properly.

STAGE 2—INITIAL PARTICIPATION IN SHOP

METHOD

For the younger, more poorly-coordinated students. Demonstrate by taking a two-by-four and hammering in a row of thumb tacks, then give each child a two-by-four, some thumb tacks, and a hammer. Press in—but not all the way—a row of tacks, then have the child hammer the tacks in the rest of the way, in left to right order.

For the older, better-coordinated students. Demonstrate by taking a two-by-four and hammering in a row of shingle nails (shingle nails are used because they have large heads and are easier to drive in than smaller-head nails), then give each child a two-by-four, some shingle nails, and a hammer. Start a series of nails in a row and have the child drive them in the rest of the way, proceeding from left to right. (The left to right sequence in nailing is primarily to give a structured approach to the nailing activity.)

RESULT

The nailing activity should be done with little difficulty by the younger children. Therefore, it will develop self-confidence and encourage them to participate further in the unit. Likewise, the activity for the older children should not prove difficult for them. You may determine if the children are hitting the nail heads squarely by checking the nails for marred or scarred heads:

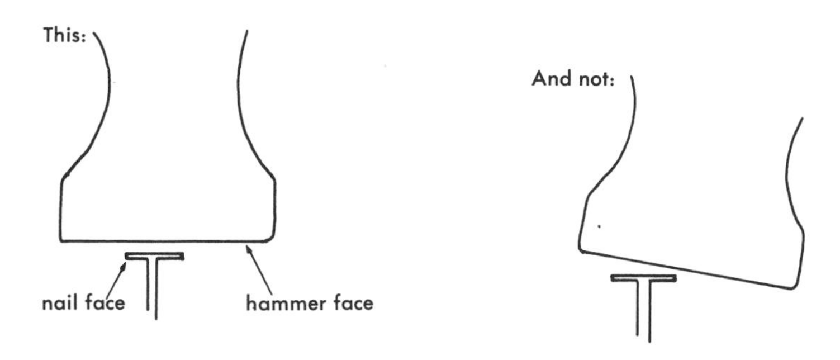

FIGURE 6-2.

Throughout this activity (and perhaps beyond it), you may have to adjust the child's hand, arm, and body position so that the hammer strikes the nail at a 90 degree angle. This is necessary to avoid having the child drive in a nail crookedly and mar the nail head and wood surface.

STAGE 3—STARTING AND REMOVING NAILS

METHOD

Starting a nail. Demonstrate by holding a nail between the thumb and forefinger of one hand, then place the nail on a two-by-four at the point where the nail is to be driven; raising the hammer a few inches above the nail, rap it lightly several times to get it started. Then call on individual students to follow this same procedure.

Removing a nail. Drive a nail one-third of its length into a two-by-four. Then turn the two-by-four so that its length is facing you. Place a small block of wood on the two-by-four behind the nail. Then place the head of the hammer on this block with the claws engaging the nail. Holding down the two-by-four with one hand, pull the nail out by gradually pushing the handle of the hammer away from the body:

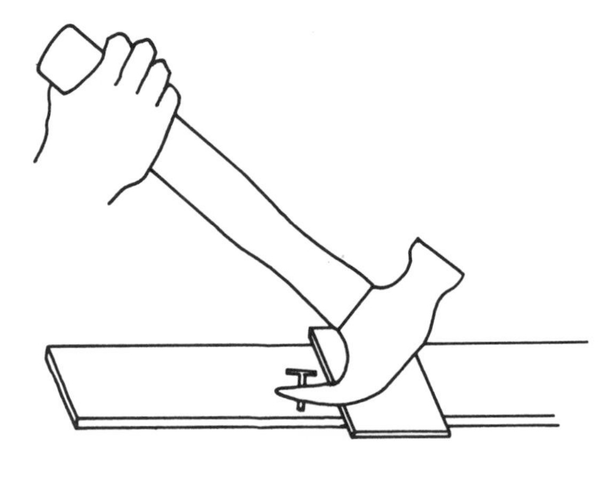

FIGURE 6-3.

RESULT

Starting a nail should not be difficult for the children; however, they might have difficulty in removing a nail. In the beginning, of course, you will supervise the children when they are engaged in this activity. They are apt to forget to use a block. You may wish to show the children what happens when a nail is removed without using a block of wood: the nail will bend, the nail hole will be made larger and the hammer will mar the wood. The children are also apt to attempt removing a nail by pulling the hammer handle forward, instead of away from the body. Therefore, you might illustrate how, by pulling the hammer forward, the handle could strike the chest.

STAGE 4—DEVELOPMENTAL ACTIVITIES (1)

METHOD

Making a tie rack. Draw a line along the length of board about one and one half inches from one side.* Then draw four or five circles along the line at least three inches apart to indicate where the nails should be placed:

*Do not have the students nail along the center of a board as it will split the wood.

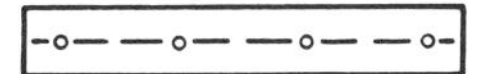

FIGURE 6-4.

Drive four or five nails about ½ an inch in on each of the circles; the nails should be even when viewed from the side, and they should be in line when viewed from the end. Have the children follow the same procedure. The tie racks may be painted with water colors.

RESULT

The children will enjoy this activity. With obvious pride, some will take their tie racks home as a gift for their fathers.*

DEVELOPMENTAL ACTIVITIES (2)

METHOD

Practice activity. Draw two lines along the length of the two-by-four, with each line about one inch from either side. Then mark three nail positions about two inches apart on each line. Nails are driven in by the student in left to right order beginning with the top line:

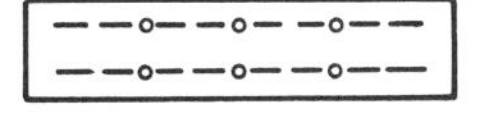

FIGURE 6-5.

RESULT

This activity may be continued over quite a long period of time; the children will not tire of it. The drawing of a line, the marking of nail holes, the even spacing of nails, and the left to right order of nailing provide a

*The children can also make a keyboard for use by the school faculty. A plain piece of wood can be sand papered (and perhaps varnished or painted) and smaller-head nails hammered in equal rows.

structured, systematic approach to an activity in which students feel secure and confident.

DEVELOPMENTAL ACTIVITIES (3)

METHOD

Practice activity. Start three nails about 1 inch apart and 1½ inches from one side of a two-by-four:

FIGURE 6-6.

Have the student drive in the three nails, then continue the row by himself. When the child finishes the first row, have him drive nails in the second row:

FIGURE 6-7.

RESULT

This activity represents a more advanced stage than the previous activity; the students are not guided by lines or by nail positions (circles), the nails are driven in closer together, and more nails are driven into the two-by-four. Some students are apt to have difficulty spacing the nails an equal distance apart. In this activity, therefore, the nails can be driven in a nail-distance apart. Have the children measure by placing a nail lengthwise on the board from the head of the last nail hammered in and marking with a pencil at the tip of the measuring nail. This is where the next nail should be driven.

DEVELOPMENTAL ACTIVITIES (4)

METHOD

Each student is given a hammer, a two-by-four, and some 1 inch nails. The students drive in the nails, spacing them evenly in one row. When the row is completed, the children are then given 1½ inch nails; these nails are driven in the next row (two rows to a board).

RESULT

It is at this stage that the children should begin to work independently of the teacher. Once the children clearly understand what they are expected to do, they should proceed with confidence and with a minimum of guidance. Some students may exhibit fatigue. If possible, they should finish nailing one row; then they can work on the second row in the next lesson.

DEVELOPMENTAL ACTIVITIES (5)

PURPOSE

1. To teach the children how to line-up pieces of wood for nailing
2. To give the children a sense of accomplishment

MATERIALS

For the simple table.

1. Two pieces of two-by-fours approximately 4 inches in length
2. One board approximately 8 inches in length, 3½ inches in width, and ¾ inch in thickness

For the small table.

1. Four pieces of two-by-fours approximately 10 inches in length
2. Three boards approximately 20 inches in length, 5 inches in width, and ¾ inch in thickness
3. Two pieces of lumber approximately 15 inches in length, 3½ inches in width, and ¾ inch in thickness

For the small chair.

1. Four two-by-fours approximately 8 inches in length
2. A board approximately nine inches by 12 inches and ¾ inch in thickness
3. Two boards 4 inches by 17½ inches, ½ inch in thickness
4. A 5½ inch by 10 inch board, ½ inch in thickness

The length of the wood used may vary as much as several inches from the sizes given above, depending on what is available to the teacher. Of course, the width and thickness can vary too.

Nails for this activity may be 1 inch or 1½ inch common nails.

METHOD

The simple table.

The piece of 8 inch board is simply nailed to the two-by-fours:

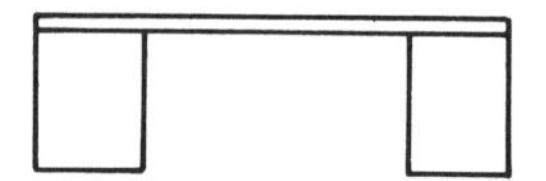

FIGURE 6-8.

Before nailing, the top piece of wood should be aligned with each two-by-four (leg). The nails should first be driven about half way down, then when the pieces are aligned, the nails can be driven all the way down. The table may be painted in water colors.

The students, of course, will need help in making the table. Particularly difficult for them will be the aligning of pieces for nailing; but this is an important woodworking skill, and the children can learn it.

The small table.

1. The two pieces of lumber are nailed to the four two-by-fours:

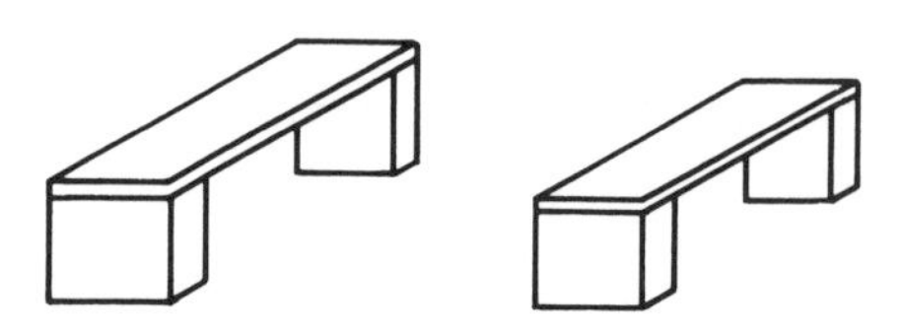

FIGURE 6-9.

2. The three pieces of board are set atop the two cross pieces and nailed:

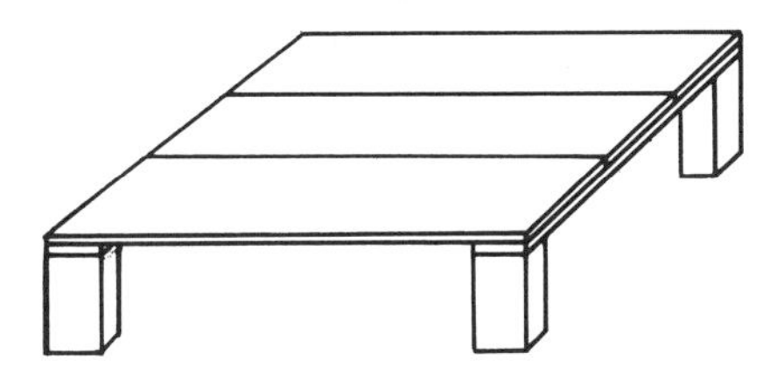

FIGURE 6-10.

3. The table may be painted with water colors, with several coats of varnish, or with two coats of any shade of stain.

Before nailing, all the pieces should be aligned. The bulk of the work should be done by students; the teacher should merely guide and assist. This table may be made after the children have learned to make the simple table.

The small chair.

1. The 9 inch by 12 inch board is set atop the four two-by-fours and nailed:

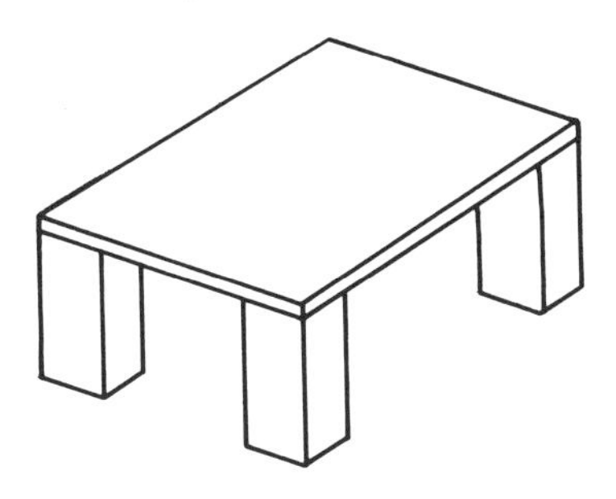

FIGURE 6-11.

2. The 5½ inch by 10 inch board is nailed across the two ½ inch boards:

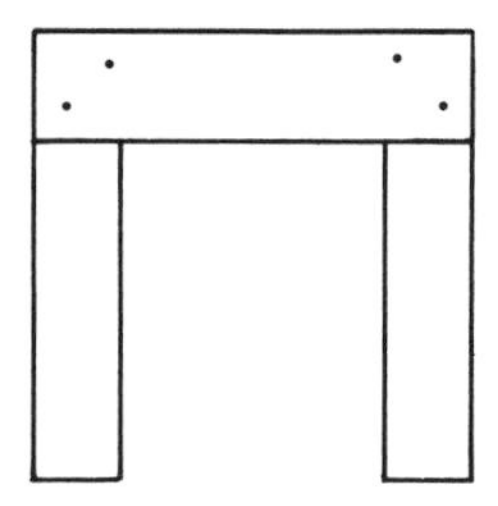

FIGURE 6-12.

3. The above section, which is the back of the chair, is nailed to two of the legs:

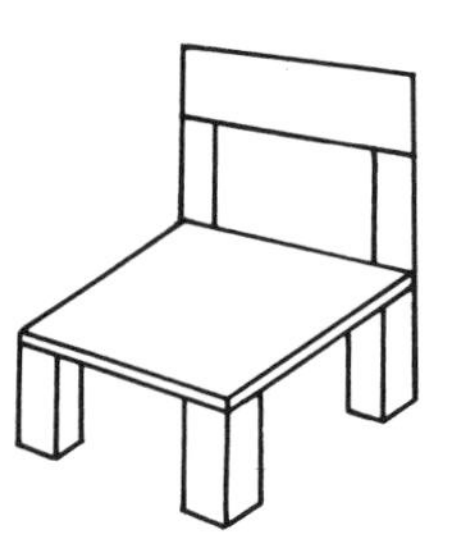

FIGURE 6-13.

4. Two coats of stain, or several coats of varnish are applied.

Of course, the children will need more assistance on this task than on the previous ones. But, the teacher should be careful to do no more than necessary. With her guidance, the children should align the pieces of wood and do the nailing. When completed, this chair should be strong enough to hold a child or an adult.

THE SCREWDRIVER

PURPOSE

1. To acquaint the children with the screwdriver, its use and proper handling

2. To provide the children with practice in using a screwdriver
3. To develop eye-hand coordination*

MATERIALS

1. A small screwdriver†
2. Small wood screws with flat or rounded heads
3. Pieces of pine or any other soft wood

METHOD

This tool may be introduced earlier, and the children may work with it at the same time that they are learning to work with a hammer. During the shop period, some of the boys and girls can work with the screwdriver and the others with the hammer. Begin by identifying the parts of the screwdriver:

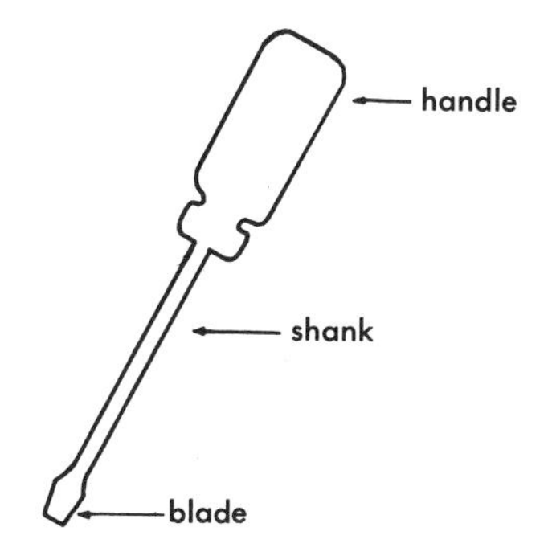

FIGURE 6-14. Screwdriver

Next demonstrate how a screw is turned. Tap a hole with a hammer and nail, then set a screw in the hole and lightly tap it with the hammer. Setting the blade in the screw slot, turn the screwdriver with one hand on the handle while the thumb and forefinger of the other hand steady the shank (so that the screwdriver blade does not slip off the slot):

*In using a screwdriver, a child is developing finer muscle coordinations, as well as eye-hand coordination, because in addition to starting and keeping the screwdriver in the screw slot, there are the combined motions of grasping, pushing, and turning.

†A star screwdriver may be easier for the younger children.

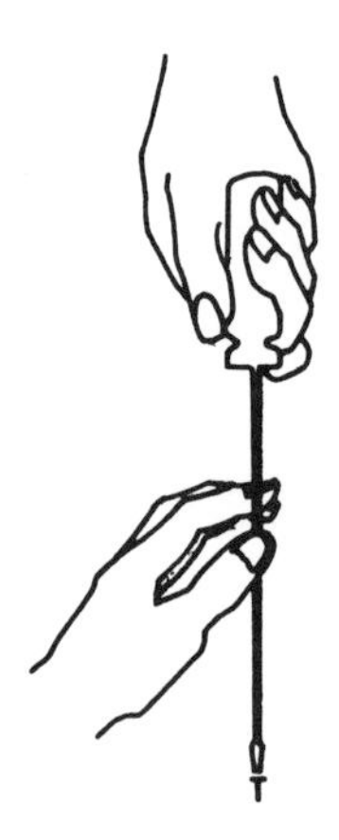

FIGURE 6-15.

Then call on one of the students. Set the screw as above and have the child turn it. Make certain the screwdriver is straight; i.e., held in a vertical position.

Pieces of pine are passed out to the students along with screwdrivers and screws. Then—under your supervision and guidance—have the children practice turning the screws. When they have turned in all the screws, have them turn out the screws. Turning out a screw involves as much eye-hand coordination as turning it in.

A game may be introduced as a developmental activity once the children have developed some proficiency in using a screwdriver. Two children with screwdrivers must turn two ½ inch screws into a board. At the teacher's signal, each child begins to turn his screw. The child who turns his screw all the way down first is the winner. A third child may play against the winner.

Pot holder racks can be made with simply a piece of wood and three screws. The girls, as well as the boys, can make these as a gift for their mothers.

CONCLUSION

Most normally intelligent children have had some experience working with a hammer by the time they start school; they are apt to know how to handle a hammer properly and are likely to have some proficiency in using it. But, for many severely retarded children handling a hammer is apt to be a totally new experience.

The children should be eager to participate in the unit. Shop work is like a bridge to normally intelligent children and adults; the activity has positive associations for severely retarded children.

What can the children achieve in the unit? The children's progress in eye-hand coordination, hand and arm strength, and proficiency in handling a hammer is suggested by their nailing performance over a period of several months. The following chart indicates the number of hammer blows it took the children to drive a 1½ inch common nail into a block of wood:

CHART 11. Nailing Performance of Six Severely Retarded Boys (January 15, 1962 to March 29, 1962)

	Jan. 15	Jan. 24	Feb. 6	Feb. 23	March 9	March 29
Jim M. 8 yrs. old	205	310	160	(unable)	216	95
Thomas F. 10 yrs. old	95	55	25	(absent)	34	52
Ronnie M. 10 yrs. old	70	63	57	35	41	25
Alan P. 12 yrs. old	25	42	57	60	15	28
Alan G. 14 yrs. old	(unable)	(unable)	(unable)	205	(absent)	(absent)
Ed K. 16 yrs. old	39	26	39	25	32	27

It will be noted that between the first and last dates the boys were tested, two boys substantially reduced the number of blows it took them to drive in the nail. Jim M. reduced the number of hammer blows to less than half what it was originally, and Ronnie M. reduced the number to almost one-third.* In addition, several of the boys learned to make the small table and chair described in the developmental activities; and they learned to handle a screwdriver with a degree of efficiency.

It is suggested that the teacher keep records of the children's participation in the unit. In nailing, she can record the number of hammer blows

*Both boys were brain-injured. It may be noted that the younger boys evidenced the greater progress in this activity.

it takes the students to drive in a nail; in work with the screwdriver, the teacher can record the time it takes the children to turn in a screw.

Although the unit is essentially designed for finer motor development, it also has semivocational or vocational implications. Through participation in the unit, the children learn to use two basic tools, the hammer and the screwdriver, and they learn basic woodworking skills. The unit, therefore, may serve as preparation for a semivocational skill, such as the assembling and nailing of crates for packaging.

Of course, the unit is of natural interest to boys, but girls may be interested in participating too. One girl in a class of severely retarded children took up a hammer on her own one day and promptly proceeded to drive nails into a block of wood; she became so adept at it that she put some of the boys "to shame."

Leather tool belts for the children can be purchased at department stores; they include a hammer, a screwdriver, a set of pliers and a folding ruler. Each belt, complete with tools, costs about three dollars.

Teachers may want to investigate the possibility of having the children, particularly the younger children, work with a special corrugated cardboard. This sturdy and versatile cardboard was originally developed as packing and shipping material, but is now being adapted for school use. Furniture and toys can be made from the cardboard.*

If the children have to work on regular tables, it is recommended that a board be placed on the tables to avoid damaging their surfaces. It is also recommended that the children wear aprons. Before starting this unit and the unit on Scouting, the teacher should consult with the parents, since the units do involve potentially dangerous activities. However, no child in the writer's class was injured in either unit.

In addition to developing finer motor coordination and some basic woodwork skills, the unit on Shop should make parents feel more secure in leaving tools within reach of their children and should bring some of the fathers closer to their children.

---

*For further information contact the Education Development Center, 55 Chapel Street, Newton, Mass. 02158; also, see David R. Babcock, "Cardboard Carpentry," *Instructor,* November 1969, and Eleanor Roth, "New Craft for Children".

Exploratory Skills

Severely retarded children seem to have little curiosity about their immediate environment. Unlike normally intelligent children, they seldom ask questions, examine objects or seem to observe much that is about them. This seems particularly true of younger severely retarded children.

Unfortunately, schools often do little to increase their awareness. The present two main areas of the curriculum—self-care and social adjustment—offer the children some awareness of their environment. Under self-care, for example, the children study safety, learn traffic precautions, traffic lights, and signs. However, for the most part, today's curriculum neglects this wonderfully interesting world in which we live.

The purpose of Exploratory Skills is to make the children more aware of the physical world. Primarily, the teacher's task in this unit is to help develop elementary sensory skills in the children.* The unit may challenge the teacher's imagination and ingenuity; however, the activities in the following pages are *merely suggestive.*

The teacher may begin with any section and, within that section, follow any order she pleases. Pestalozzi sounded the keynote that may well be followed by the teacher. The father of modern elementary education opposed verbal teaching, especially in science, "Let him (the teacher)

*Refer to the work and ideas of Dr. Montessori in sensory development.

realize that she (nature) is the real teacher. . . . If a bird should sing or an insect should crawl on a leaf, stop your conversation immediately; the bird and insect are teaching the child more and better."

AWAKENING AND DEVELOPING CURIOSITY

PLANTS

1. Have the children bring in small plants. Encourage them to examine the plants. Point out the roots, the stems, the leaves, and the flowers (if any).
2. The children can plant seeds in coffee cans or jars. Have the children water the seeds each day. Encourage them to observe the growth of the plants.
3. Have the children cut pictures of plants from magazines. Help them to group the pictures: plants that have flowers, those without flowers, plants that grow in the earth, in the water, in the desert, etc. The pictures can be mounted on the bulletin board, and the children can make their own Plant Picture Books.
4. Perhaps, the children can be taken on a visit to a botanical garden, a nursery or a flower shop.

LAND ANIMALS

1. The children can bring hamsters or other small animals to class. Let them care for the class pets each day.
2. Have the children learn—through looking and observing—the answers to such questions as:
   a. What sort of food does the pet eat?
   b. What does the pet have for covering?
   c. Has the pet a tail?
   d. How many feet, eyes, ears, etc, does the pet have?
   e. How many toes are there on the back feet? How many on the front feet? How does the animal move its feet to walk?
   f. How does it use its paws (to hold food, to clean itself)?
   g. Are the animal's legs long or short? Are the back legs the same as the front ones?
   h. What color eyes does it have? Are the eyes in front of the head or at the sides?

   i. Are the pet's ears long or short? What shape are they?
   j. What sort of mouth does it have? Does it have teeth? If it has teeth, are they sharp, flat or both?
3. The children can cut out pictures of different land animals from magazines. Help the children group the pictures: animals that have fur, animals that have hair, animals that carry burdens for people, animals that live in the desert, *etc.* The pictures can be mounted on the bulletin board; the students can also make their own picture books of land animals, with the names of the animals written under the pictures.
4. The children may be taken on a visit to a zoo or a farm.

WATER ANIMALS

1. Have the students set up a classroom aquarium. A regular fish tank can be used or, if one is not available, a pie dish or bowl. Place sand, pebbles, and a few stones at the bottom of the container (a water plant may be added too). Fill the container about two-thirds full with tap water,* then inside place small fish—tropical, goldfish or sunfish.
2. Let the children observe and care for the fish each day.
3. Each student can set up his own aquarium. Glass jars may be used. A small fish is placed in each jar. The student's name is taped to the jar, and he or she is responsible for the fish.
4. Through observation, have the children answer the following questions:
   a. How do fish swim?
   b. Do they have feet?
   c. What sort of food do they eat?
   d. What do they have for covering?
5. The children can be taken on a visit to an aquarium or a pet shop.

AIR ANIMALS

1. The children can set up a bird feeding station outside the classroom. It may consist of simply a tray which is set on the window sill.†

---

*If the tap water is chlorinated or fluoridated, allow it to stand a day or two before placing the fish.

†The birds may be afraid to come to the window tray at first. If so, a bird table may be set up a little distance away from the windows, preferably near a tree.

2. Have the children place food and water on the tray each day. The food might include bread crumbs, pieces of apples, nuts, wild bird seeds, sunflower seeds or suet.
3. The children can observe the birds that come to the feeding station, and they can learn the names of the birds.
4. Have the children learn the answers to the following questions by their observation of live birds and by their study of bird pictures:
   a. How do the birds move on the ground? Do they hop? Do they walk?
   b. How many feet do they have? What sort of feet do they have? How many claws?
   c. What sort of covering do birds have?
   d. Do birds have tails?
   e. What sort of mouth do birds have? Are the beaks long or short?

HOMEWORK ASSIGNMENTS

Assigning one item at a time, ask the students to be prepared to tell the class about such things as the following:

1. The color of their house
2. The color of their room
3. The color of their mother's and father's (brother's and sister's) eyes
4. How many traffic lights they pass on their school bus
5. How many gas stations they pass on the way to school
6. Which is the tallest building they pass on the way to school
7. Which is the prettiest tree they pass on the way to school
8. Which is the largest room in their house
9. Were there stars out last night? Could they see the stars from the windows of their room?

A Final Note

> "Develop a sense of humor. There will be times when to relieve the buildup of tensions you will need to laugh or cry, and laughter is the better medicine." *(Clara M. Chaney and Newell C. Kephart, Motoric Aids to Perceptual Training)*

Teaching severely retarded children is not a grim task. In fact, particularly in a class with dowsyn children, there can be wonderful moments of humor for the students and teacher. These moments are important in lightening the tension and boredom of routine. The following anecdotes are based on the writer's experience.

Alan P., a dowsyn boy, was the brightest in the class. He was short, hair-slicked, brown-eyed, pug-nosed, and a "politician." One day when the class was passing by the school cafeteria he asked me to stop a moment; I did. Alan walked into the cafeteria through one door and fifteen seconds later came out another door munching on a hot dog. The conversation that followed went likes this:

"Where did you get this?"

"The lady gave it to me."

"Did you ask her for it?"

"Nope."

I went inside the cafeteria and spoke to the cafeteria worker.

"Did Alan ask for the hot dog?"

"Not exactly."

"How . . . ?"

"He came in here, said hello, said I was a nice lady— that he likes me very much—and said the hot dogs smelled so good. So . . . ."

Alan was fond of my wife. (The class had been to my home.) Alan often wrote her love letters, simple notes, such as, "Dear Fanny, I love you. Will you marry me? Love, Alan."

I tried to point out to Alan that she was married to me. (He knew this, of course.) After Alan placed such notes on my desk, the conversation usually went like this:

"What's this?"

"A love note to Fanny."

(Pretending I was shocked.) "To Fanny?"

"Yep."

"But she's married."

"I want to marry her."

"But she's my wife!"

"I don't care. I love her, and I . . . ."

"This is against the rules. I will have to report this to the proper authorities."

"Tell the principal," the other boys in the class would call out.

"This will be exhibit 'A'," (folding the paper and placing it in my jacket).

". . . Please, give it to Fanny."

". . . Well, all right; but no more notes."

Then there was Ed K., a strapping teenage dowsyn boy. He was blond, very fair, and very proud. Ed apparently had acted as a straw-boss for the previous teacher. When I first took over the class, I quickly learned that I had to be careful of what I said, for if I gave even a hint of displeasure the guilty party was immediately threatened by annihilation from Ed's fist smacking down on the poor victim's head.

One day, another boy committed a minor infraction of a class rule. Teasing him, I warned him that the paddle over the blackboard (which I had inherited and which was now decorative), would be used if he wasn't careful. No sooner said than Ed had the paddle firmly in hand and was chasing the culprit around the room yelling, "Come on. Take it like a man!"

Ed liked to be a leader. When we formed a Boy Scout patrol, Ed was the patrol leader. We made a patrol flag; it was Ed who always carried the flag.

One day we got carried away with the spirit of the activity and our marching took us right out the classroom (I always left the door open) and into the hall. Down the hall we marched, seven boys happily following their patrol leader (who proudly bore the patrol flag), followed by me. We continued down the hall past the principal's office. He stepped out of his office as we passed and stood openmouthed, staring in disbelief, as the patrol filed past him. I murmered something as I went past him, then picked up my heels to catch up with the onward-marching patrol—its banner waving on high.

Tommy F. was the class favorite. He was dowsyn, short, chubby, round-faced and impish, with a quick grin. Tommy was quiet much of the time; on the few occasions when he spoke, it was strictly for laughs, which he cultivated like a ham-comedian.

One day, while checking over his homework, I inquired about his mother. He didn't answer. I asked again:

"How's your mother, Tommy?"

". . . Old witch."

(Pretending I didn't see the connection) "No, Tom, I mean your mother. How's your mother?"

". . . Old witch." He grinned.

(Pretending to be aghast) "Tommy! You don't really mean that. Now, be serious. How is your charming mother?"

"Old witch."

"Young man, I'm surprised at you. That is bad, very bad." Tommy grinned again. "Now unless you immediately apologize for saying that about your lovely mother, I'll . . . ."

"Fresh!"

Tommy was the laziest boy in the class. One day he feigned illness so that he wouldn't have to do any writing. His illness-act was strictly from a grade "z" movie. Tommy, sitting at his desk during the writing lesson, suddenly groaned, brought a hand to his forehead, held his throat, coughed, then came to his feet, tottered, and steadied himself on the desk as his knees started to buckle.

With a straight face, I asked, "Tom, is something wrong?"

Tommy answered by swaying on his feet. Alan ran to him. Tommy gingerly collapsed in Alan's arms.

Alan asked, "Should I take him to the nurse, Teacher?"

"I don't know. Tommy, what's wrong? Speak to me."

Tommy coughed (a consumptive-sounding cough). "This looks and sounds serious," I said. I emphasized that last word. But Tom didn't bat an eye.

"All right. Take him to the nurse, Alan." I went to my desk. "Take this note with you." I wrote: *Tom is playing Hamlet today. Send him back in five minutes.*

Leaning heavily on Alan, Tom moved out of the room. He waved a feeble goodbye to us, then buried a grin on Alan's shoulder.